Crossroads School Library
500 DeBaliviere Ave
St Louis MO 63112

FOOD
The Struggle to Sustain the
Human Community

FOOD

The Struggle to Sustain the Human Community

by
Jake Goldberg

FRANKLIN WATTS
A Division of Grolier Publishing
New York London Hong Kong Sydney
Danbury, Connecticut

Photographs ©: Affordable Photo Stock: 169 (Francis E. Caldwell); Archive Photos: 34 (Popperfoto), 160 (Reuters/Mike Segar), 37, 51, 80, 96; Corbis-Bettmann: 24, 46, 68, 75, 83, 88; Envision: 102 (Jean Higgins), 18 (Steven Needham); Gamma-Liaison, Inc.: 122 (Wesley Hitt), 15 (Keith Lanpher), 111 (Morimoto), cover bottom (Daniel Nichols), 144 (Scott Daniel Peterson); Monkmeyer Press: 132 (Randy Matusow); North Wind Picture Archives: 27, 41, 57, 163; Photo Researchers: 149 (M. Courtney Clarke), 175 (Fasol/Explorer), cover top right (Jeff Greenberg), 186 (National Audubon Society/Jerome Wexler), 166 (M. P. Kahl), 179 (National Audubon Society/Leonard Lee Rue III), 11 (Lawrence Migdale), cover top left (Leonide Prince), 131 (Charles D. Winters); Tony Stone Images: 13 (James Balog), 105 (Paul Chesley), 115 (Darrell Gulin), 9 (Paul Redman), 6 (Jay S. Simon), 177 (Oliver Strewe), 170 (Robert Van Der Hilst), 194 (Randy Wells).

Interior design and page makeup: Claire Fontaine

Visit Franklin Watts on the Internet at: http://publishing.grolier.com

Library of Congress Cataloging-in-Publication Data

Goldberg, Jake, 1943–
Food : the struggle to sustain the human community / by Jake Goldberg
p. cm.
Includes bibliographical references and index.
Summary: Discusses the history of food, its production, and the political ramifications of its dissemination and consumption.
ISBN 0-531-11411-2
1. Food—History—Juvenile literature. 2. Food supply—History—Juvenile literature.
[1. Food. 2. Food supply. 3. Agriculture.] I. Title.
TX357.G574 1999
641.3'09—dc21   98-28225
                                                          CIP
                                                          AC

©1999 by Jake Goldberg
All rights reserved. Published simultaneously in Canada.
1 2 3 4 5 6 7 8 9 0 R 08 07 06 05 04 03 02 00 99

Contents

	Introduction	7
One	The Origin of Food	20
Two	The Development of Agriculture	33
Three	Food and Civilization	71
Four	Food Production Today	108
Five	Hunger	141
Six	The Future of Food	174
	Source Notes	199
	For Further Information	200
	Index	204

A field of quinoa in Colorado

Introduction

Nobody is qualified to become a statesman who is entirely ignorant of the problem of wheat.
—Socrates

This is a book about food, but it is not a cookbook. There are no recipes to be found here. It is not a restaurant guide. It does not contain a new diet. Nor is it a book about the science of nutrition, digestion, or metabolism. We will talk briefly about nutrition and digestion, and about proteins, fats, carbohydrates, vitamins, and minerals, and how the body uses them. And we will get that subject out of the way quickly, right here in the introduction to this book, because it has very little to do with how people really *experience* food. People experience food as that which tastes good and satisfies the gnawing hunger they feel when they haven't eaten. They experience food as that which gives them the strength and health to carry on day after day, as something so necessary to their well-being that they will make enormous efforts, apply the keenest intelligence, cooperate with each other, or even kill each other, to obtain it. The consumption of food is also an act of pleasure and fulfillment that sustains the bonds of family and renews the commitment to work and to participate in social activity.

The Experience of Food

It is important to bear in mind how people really experience food, because for most of their history human beings have had very little understanding of the principles of nutrition. The first hunters did not set off to bring down a load of protein. Nor did the first farmers go out to reap a harvest of carbohydrates. What drives our search for food is not the desire for a healthy, balanced diet—and certainly few enough people in human history have enjoyed that—but anticipation of the sense of satisfaction and fullness, the feeling of strength and robustness, and the sensation of flavorfulness that comes from eating. To these basic cravings we have attached deep emotions about the nurturing of our loved ones, the survival of our social group, and the continuance of our way of life. These are as much matters of human psychology as they are matters of nutrition, and throughout history it has often been our desires and prejudices, rather than our nutritional requirements, that have determined what and how we eat. Nutrition is important because, in the long run, only those people who survive disease, malnutrition, starvation, and poisoning are able to pass on their food preferences to the next generation. Nevertheless, until very recently at least, the motivating force behind our food-producing activities has been our yearning to satisfy our hunger and to promote our sense of well-being. Improved health has come almost as an afterthought. We eat because food tastes good and makes us feel good.

There is a crude correlation between the foods that are healthy and nourishing for us and the foods we desire. Our tongues are designed to help us find the right foods. Generally, what is sweet is edible; if something is sour or bitter, it might be dangerous to eat. The olfactory nerves in our noses add further subtleties to our sense of taste and tell us quite a bit about the state of freshness or putrefaction of foods. If we have been deprived of essential nutrients, our bodies sometimes generate cravings for the foods that contain them. But on the whole, taste rather than biological necessity has shaped our eating habits. Good-tasting food is so important to us that

Food not only nourishes us but cements the bonds of our family or social group.

we have devoted enormous energies to expanding the variety of available foods, to experimenting with their preparation and cooking, and to broadening the spectrum of available flavors and spices for the delight of the human palette.

Food is also experienced as that which staves off death. It allows us to pursue, and gives meaning to, all the other human activities we regard as important. To deprive someone of food is not simply to kill that person, but to render a judgment on that person's importance in the world, and on that person's interests and desires. The distribution of food in a society determines who has been raised up and who has been cast down, who shall enjoy the pleasures of living and who shall be deprived of them, whose actions and ideas will prevail, who shall lead and who shall follow, and who shall determine the shape of the future.

Food in History

All this has made a lot of history and may in fact be said to lie at the root of many other changes in human affairs, and that is the subject of this book. The search for food has made us what we are as human beings and social animals. It has shaped our history and our culture, determined the structure of our societies and governments, and influenced how we think about our gods and our world. The growth of the food supply has always been the signal for increasing human numbers, so that food is the foundation upon which we build our complex social relationships and our civilization. Surplus food ensures social stability; a scarcity of food, or famine, produces chaos and revolution. It is no coincidence that democratic societies, the societies that allow individual human beings the greatest freedom of action, are also the societies in which food is most abundant. And food preferences have in turn been shaped by culture and class. What we eat classifies us as rich or poor, privileged or common, sophisticated or dull, superior or inferior. The story of the search for food is much larger, more complicated, and more interesting than the search for a healthy diet, even though adequate nutrition is the underlying problem that must always be solved.

Food creates history because it is the basis of all material wealth. All that we have, we have made with our own hands, or with tools and machines of our own making. To make these things, we have to relinquish some or all of the time and labor we would otherwise have to spend searching for food. Others must now provide food for us by producing more food than they

Food can be a sign of wealth or poverty, and sometimes eating food can be fun.

need for themselves. The number of people who can be freed from the work of producing food to build a complex civilization depends upon the amount of surplus food available to feed them. If we want clothing, weavers and tailors must be fed; if we want shelter, there must be food for masons and carpenters. If we want security, there must be food for generals and their armies. If we want lawyers and accountants, then someone must feed them. We pay all these people money for their products and services, so it would appear that money is true wealth. But if that money couldn't buy food, it would be largely useless. What made the emperors of China "the sons of heaven," what filled their palaces with magnificent jade carvings and exquisite silk screen paintings, what adorned their chambers with elegant calligraphy and carved sandalwood, can all be found in a bowl of rice.

In the past, control of the surplus food supply conferred upon rulers enormous political power. In ancient times, rulers kept their vaults full of gold and silver, but they also maintained control of the granaries. The connection among food and wealth and power has been submerged in modern western civilization, where food is cheap and plentiful and available everywhere, and where most of us seem to devote our energies to the pursuit of other things. In the United States, for example, fewer than 5 million people, only about 2 percent of the population, work on farms and provide food for the other 248 million people. There are fewer farmers than there are unemployed. For most Americans, the struggle to find food is hidden beneath the struggle to educate oneself, to find a suitable trade or profession, and to earn an income to buy it. But it remains a fact that the underlying source of our wealth is the fuel of human labor—food. If all the farmers and fishermen and breeders of livestock were to stop their activities tomorrow, in a few short months we would understand the true value of food, and nothing else would matter very much.

Nutritional Requirements

What is food? What is it that human beings need to eat? They need, first of all, carbohydrates, complex molecules of carbon, hydrogen, and oxygen atoms classified as starches and sugars. Our digestive system converts starches and complex sugars into glucose, a simple sugar that is the fuel for all cellular activity. The atoms of the glucose molecule, like all molecules, are held together by bonds of electromagnetic energy. When the molecule is broken apart, that energy is released in the form of heat, which causes other chemical reactions and sustains the life of the cell. So carbohydrates are a source of energy and constitute most of the food that we eat. Many foods have heavy concentrations of sugars and starches, but people get the

Wheat is one of the most important grains in the world. It is used for flour that, in turn, goes into making many foods.

bulk of their carbohydrates by eating the seeds of about a half dozen species of grass—rye, oats, barley, millet, sorghum—and the three most important seeds in the world—wheat, rice, and corn. These seeds are ground into the flour and meal from which we make all our breads and pastas, our cakes and cookies and puddings, our udon and soba noodles, and our tortillas, tacos, and enchiladas. They are also used to make our breakfast cereals. Rice is not generally milled, but eaten in its seed form. One species of corn, sweet corn, is also eaten in this form. Corn appears in our foods in many different forms, such as corn oil, corn syrup, and cornstarch. It is also a principal source of food for the animals we breed, so we consume corn indirectly when we eat meat. Other foods, such as fruits and vegetables, beans, peas, and root crops like potatoes, manioc, and yams, are also rich in carbohydrates. We can't live on carbohydrates alone, but we must continually consume large quantities of them to provide energy for our bodies. The result of an insufficient intake of carbohydrates is not one of the diseases that results from a dietary deficiency, but simple starvation. The continuous need of human beings for energy to carry on the daily activities of life makes carbohydrate-rich foods into *staples*, basic foods for which there is a wide and regular demand. Wheat, rice, corn, and potatoes alone supply the world with half its carbohydrates. Without these cereal grains and starchy legumes and lentils, there would be far fewer people in the world, and no civilization as we know it.

We also need proteins. Proteins are molecules in which the carbon, hydrogen, and oxygen atoms of carbohydrates are combined with nitrogen, sulfur, and some other elements to form compounds that make up the permanent structures of our cells and many of the complex chemicals essential to biological processes. Proteins are made up of amino acids. The human body builds thousands of proteins from different combinations of nineteen amino acids. Eleven of these amino acids can be synthesized by the body from other substances, but eight of them—the so-called essential amino acids—cannot be manufactured in the body and must be taken in

Raising cattle for protein is an expensive venture, since large amounts of grain are used to feed the livestock.

from foods that already contain them. An example of a protein would be hemoglobin, which transports oxygen through the bloodstream. Hemoglobin is made up of 287 uniquely arranged amino acid groups.

Many good sources of carbohydrates, including some cereal grains, are also good sources of protein. Wheat is the grain richest in protein, containing between 7 percent and 15 percent protein, depending on the variety. Brown rice contains about 8 percent protein; corn somewhat less than that. Beans, especially soybeans, and peas and nuts are rich in protein. But the richest sources of protein are the muscle tissues of animals and fish. There has been considerable debate about the wisdom of obtaining protein from meat. Because of the large amounts of feed grains needed to raise cattle, chickens, hogs, and sheep, meat is a very expensive form of protein. In the United States alone, 80 percent of the huge corn crop we produce is fed to livestock. This may not be a wise trade-off in areas of the world where there is barely enough grain to feed the people. Until fairly recently, the accepted wisdom was that at least two of the essential amino acids needed by human beings could be obtained only by eating meat and fish. In the 1970s, Frances Moore Lappé, in her revolutionary book *Diet for a Small Planet*, argued that the right combination of grains and vegetables could provide all the essential amino acids in a cheaper and healthier diet. Meat, however, remains a popular source of protein in the industrialized world. Necessary or not, people who eat meat and fish are generally larger, taller, and more robust than those who do not eat meat, and throughout history meat-eating has been a sign of affluence.

Human beings must also consume a certain amount of fats and oils. These provide essential fatty acids, and, under some circumstances, fat is converted into an energy food. Red meat, as well as the meat from poultry like ducks and geese, and certain fish are good sources of fat and oils. Butter is made from converted animal fat. Another good source are oilseeds like sunflower, safflower, and sesame, as well as certain legumes like peanuts and soybeans. If one eats too much fat and the body cannot metabolize it fast enough, obesity results. This can lead to heart disease and other ailments. Nevertheless, some fat is necessary in the human diet.

We also need vitamins and minerals. Vitamins are complex molecules that are necessary to many chemical reactions in the body, and minerals are heavier atoms—iron, calcium, phosphorus, and others—that not only assist in chemical reactions but form essential building blocks for the protein structures. They are essential in many subtle ways, and if you try to do without a proper mix of vitamins and minerals, you will know it soon enough. Lack of sufficient vitamin A is the main cause of blindness in children. A vitamin C deficiency produces the disease known as scurvy. Lack of iron produces anemia, lack of calcium produces brittle bones, and lack of iodine produces slow mental development and goiter.

We also need fiber. Fiber consists of molecules that are very tough to break down, and the human digestive system can't really extract nutrients from them. But by continually passing large amounts of fiber through the digestive system, it is kept functioning properly, since it was designed to handle a certain bulk of indigestible material. The stalks and leaves of vegetables contain fiber in the form of indigestible cellulose, and we eat our salads and fiber-rich foods so that our digestive organs can get exercise.

We also need water, lots of it. It makes up more than 95 percent of our bodies. It provides the fluid medium within our cells that allows chemical reactions to take place, because chemicals dissolve in it and mix more easily. It is also essential as a coolant. A human being with some stored body fat might survive for three or four weeks without food, but it would take only three or four days to die of thirst. Water is also essential to the growth of our crops. All the great ancient civilizations are to be found near rivers.

Of all the available foods in the world, only one—breast milk—provides everything a human being needs to eat. Since we don't remain babies for very long, we have to become very clever in our adult strategies for obtaining the proper balance of foods. In industrialized nations such as the United States, we are taught about proper daily diet with metaphors like the "food pyramid." At the base we begin with a broad foundation of bread, cereal, pasta, or rice. We build upon that with solid blocks of fruits and vegetables. Next come meat, poultry, fish, beans, eggs, and nuts, as well as milk and cheese, and the pyramid is topped off with fatty foods and sweets. The nutritionist assumes a world in which there is widespread availability of several cultivated cereal grains, large numbers of livestock, abundant fisheries,

*The food pyramid shows a foundation of bread, cereal, pasta, and rice.
Then we build upon that foundation with other foods.*

great quantities of vegetables and warm-weather fruits, and, in general, access to a broadly diversified agricultural system.

Our ability, however, in some modern societies, to even talk about acquiring all the foods necessary for a balanced diet, presupposes a high level of social organization, a scientific research establishment, advanced agricultural technology, a food-production system that adequately rewards the producers and is democratically responsive to consumers, and considerable global economic power. For much of human history, and in many places in the world today, societies did not and do not enjoy all these advantages, and they have suffered accordingly. The struggle for food has been an intense struggle, and it involves the development of the right social and economic institutions as well as knowledge of the right foods. How those institutions develop and function, in modern times as well as in the past, is the real subject of this book.

Chapter One
The Origin of Food

Let's begin with a short history of time, the time, that is, during which food became a concern for living things. Between 4.5 billion and 4 billion years ago, the relentless bombardment of meteorites and the violent volcanic activity began to subside on Earth, and the planet began to cool down and solidify. With a cooler Earth, the rains no longer evaporated as soon as they fell, and the oceans formed, collecting in the low-lying basins and exposing the land masses. It is from this time that geologists date the oldest known solid rocks.

The primeval oceans were full of dissolved metals and salts eroded from the rocks, along with carbon and hydrogen compounds absorbed from the gases of the atmosphere. The sun bathed the surface of the ocean with heat energy. The laws of organic chemistry went to work and some fairly large and complex molecules were formed. Sometime between 4 billion and 3.5 billion years ago, some of these molecules developed the ability to replicate themselves. When a burst of light or heat damaged or ripped apart one of these molecules, the fragments bonded with new atoms in the sea in a way that reproduced the same molecule, or one very close to it. By a process that remains very mysterious to us, these molecules multiplied in number and bonded into larger and larger groups. They had no thought of improving their chances of survival in this way. They had no thought at all. They were simply combining and recombining chemically with the atoms surrounding them—and preserving and expanding their structure as an unintended by-product of the process, just as a crystal grows.

The larger structures, however, began to be affected by a new force of nature. When they replicated themselves, the new structures were not always exact copies. Soon there was a great variety of these structures, some of which functioned better than others at building themselves or withstanding the surrounding environment.

These superior structures were "selected" by nature to thrive and reproduce. A sphere of linked molecules, for example, would efficiently expose all the molecules to the surrounding chemical mix. It would add strength and resistance to changes in water pressure, and certain valuable chemicals might even be trapped inside the sphere by diffusion through the molecular layer. There, in an improved chemical mix, new molecules might replicate more efficiently. The interior of the sphere had a different composition from the sea outside, and chemical activity inside the structure generated heat energy for molecular repair. Repeating a successful design, some molecules might form smaller spheres within the larger sphere, and within these smaller spheres, some chemical processes became localized, working symbiotically with other molecular groups to preserve the whole structure.

At some point, the whole became greater than the sum of its parts, the structure more stable and longer lasting than any of its constituent molecules, the chemistry reorganized to preserve the greater geometry rather than the individual molecular bonds. These first self-replicating biochemical machines marked the origin of life on Earth.

The First Organisms

About 3.5 billion years ago, the first single-celled living organisms appeared. They were little more than tiny bubbles of complex molecules, but they were able to maintain their structure against the chaos of the surrounding environment. They formed in the shallow seas of the continental shelves. They needed the protection of the waters against the destructive power of cosmic and solar radiation, but they also needed shallow waters in order to absorb some of that radiation. That was because they contained a rather remarkable molecule known as chlorophyll. The chlorophyll molecule uses the light energy of sunlight to split apart molecules of water, discard the oxygen, and combine the hydrogen in them with carbon dioxide to form glucose. Glucose is a sugar molecule that can be spun into long chains known as polymers, which preserved the living structure of these first cells. These first living things were blue-green algae—plants—and they literally ate the sunlight. The electromagnetic energy of the sun, in the range of visible light, converted by plants into heat energy and used to break up other compounds and reconstitute them into nutrients, was and is, then and now, the first food, and so plants are known as the primary producers.

Nothing much seemed to be happening for a very long time, but actually a profound change was now taking place. These single-celled organisms were multiplying all across the surface of the oceans, and some of them were discovering survival advantages in forming larger, bound groups of multicellular design. At the interface between sea and air, they took carbon dioxide and other gases out of the atmosphere and replaced them with oxygen. The oxygen content of the atmosphere began to build up, and high up in the atmosphere these oxygen molecules began to absorb some of the destructive solar and cosmic radiation coming from space. They broke up and re-formed into the molecule we call ozone, creating a protective layer of ozone and opening up the land and the air to the expansion of life. These first living organisms had changed the composition of Earth's atmosphere and terraformed the planet, creating the conditions for their own further evolution.

But molecular oxygen is highly reactive, and it was poisonous to these first living organisms, so they remained in their protective ocean environment for a long time. By blind and dumb evolutionary experiment, however, nature discovered that certain larger, more complex, and more stable multicellular creatures could handle the reactive power of oxygen. They were capable of taking in larger amounts of raw materials, maintaining a higher rate of metabolism, and using oxygen to build new structures and adopt new strategies, such as nervous response and movement, in order to feed. A threshold was crossed as many living organisms abandoned photosynthesis and learned how to burn their food in an oxygen fire.

A Food Revolution

This was a food revolution of major proportions. The new organisms, unlike algae or plankton, couldn't just lie around, floating on the surface of the sea, basking in the sunlight for a meal. Their oxygen metabolism required more energy than could be obtained in this way. The new organisms had to move around in their environment, find their food, perhaps pursue it, then ingest it, and finally digest it. The new organisms were *eaters*. The lifestyle of the eaters involved continuous mechanical and chemical activity, and required a lot of energy. Eaters spent most of their time looking for food, had to be successful at finding it, and had to be able to break down the food into bits and pieces that their cells could use. Eaters also had to reproduce enough of their own kind so that they would not all be eaten by other eaters. In the struggle of the eaters, it was a great advantage when a genetic mutation produced a creature with a slightly improved way of accomplishing any of these tasks.

This food revolution occurred about 600 million years ago. It is called the Cambrian explosion, and it introduced the long Paleozoic and

Millions of years ago, dinosaurs were among Earth's inhabitants.

Mesozoic eras, which lasted from 600 million to 65 million years ago and saw the emergence of so many new forms of life. The evolutionary power of natural selection was unleashed, and living creatures increased in complexity and diversity and size. The oceans filled with fish, and plant life crept onto the land. Insects appeared, as well as amphibious creatures that could live in both dry and watery environments. Then came the reptiles, the dinosaurs, the birds, and the first small mammals. The eaters had complex digestive organs designed to break down and rework other organic materials, and so they fed on other living organisms, and are now known as consumers rather than producers of food. Organisms that ate the plants are known as primary consumers, and organisms that fed upon these plant-eaters are known as secondary consumers. In this way, over time, a complex series of food chains were formed, with one organism depending for its existence on the abundance of other organisms, and the death of some being the source of life for others. Living things became interested in one another in the deadliest way. A powerful new force was added to the evolutionary equation, the adaptive struggle between predator and prey. This accelerated the development of new biological systems and behavior patterns for eating or avoiding being eaten—more intelligence and sensory awareness, more mobility, more reproductive power, and more protection and nurturing for immature organisms.

About 65 million years ago, at the end of the Cretaceous period, a major cataclysm of some kind killed off the dinosaurs and many other forms of life. This was the beginning of the Cenozoic era, our current geological era. Suddenly Earth was safe and roomy enough for the small mammals to expand their range and numbers, to grow in size, and to come down out of the safety of the treetops and search for food elsewhere. About 2 million years ago, Earth entered the Pleistocene epoch, the epoch of the ice ages, when the planet would periodically cool and huge glacial sheets would descend from the poles over the former temperate zones. This was a tremendous hardship for living creatures, but mammals developed thick coats of fur and learned how to store food in their bodies as fat. The water trapped in the ice sheets had come from the oceans, and sea levels during an ice age might fall by as much as 500 feet (152 m), exposing large areas of the continental shelves, so that the land lost to the glaciers was partly compensated for by the exposure of new coastal areas and land bridges. The land bridges provided migration routes for animals from continent to continent, and the new coastal regions became fertile alluvial plains when the glaciers receded, leaving behind them a torrent of new rivers. In the long interglacial periods between the ices ages, the climate was warm and mild, much warmer and milder than it is today, and plants and animals thrived in the new forests and grasslands that spread from the tropics to the temperate zones of the planet.

The First Humans

The Pleistocene epoch is also our epoch, for at some point just before the ice ages arrived, a little more than 2 million years ago, the first distinctly human creature, *Australopithecus afarensis*, stood up and walked out of the African forests. The australopithecines had large jaws and small brains, about one-third the size of the modern human brain. Their bodies were short and small, and probably looked thin and hungry most of the time. They ate almost everything they could find—seeds, fruits, nuts, roots, insects, worms, grubs, snails, and small lizards. Their teeth show that they were also meat-eaters, but in the beginning they were no match for the other predators of the grasslands—the big cats—and for the most part they stayed hidden in the background, waiting for the larger predators to move on, and then competing with other scavengers for the dead carcasses. Here there was tasty fat and gristle, and the bones were cracked open to get at the nutritious marrow. The meat made the australopithecines stronger and more vital, and soon they learned to hunt as well as scavenge, using stones and animal bones and horns as their weapons.

Under the intense environmental pressure of the coming and waning of the ice sheets, the human species grew larger and more intelligent, and with increasing intelligence came language and complex social interactions that encouraged cooperative activity. By the time Cro-Magnon, or modern *Homo sapiens*, appeared on the scene approximately 40,000 years ago, as the ice began to recede at the end of the Fourth Glacial Period, humans

Early hunters pursued wildlife, including the huge woolly mammoth, for food.

were full-fledged hunters and fishers as well as gatherers and scavengers. They were smart enough to take on even the huge woolly mammoths that roamed the landscape. For the most part, they hunted deer, antelope, giraffe, wildebeest, wildfowl, wild cattle called aurochs, wild horses, and wild goats, sheep, and pigs. Their new meat diet was rich in protein, and people became healthier and more vigorous. Humans also became dependent upon meat as a source of salt. From the hides of animals, clothing was made, and ancient artists made paints from their blood and fat and drew pictures of the animals they ate on the walls of caves.

For most of their time on Earth, humans have been hunter-gatherers. Life was nomadic as people followed the animals they hunted, and both animals and humans spread out from their origins into the temperate zones as the glaciers receded. Hunting was difficult and dangerous work, and often unsuccessful unless the hunters were organized and disciplined and used every trick they could think of. The entire clan hunted as a group, and every member—young, old, and sick—received a share of the kill. There was an intense interest in tools and hunting weapons. The bow and arrow was invented, as well as the spear and harpoon, the stone sling, the poison-tipped arrow, the fish hook and fishing net, and the pit trap. Humans had learned from other predators how to tire out and capture faster animals by hunting in teams and herding them into ambushes. Wolves were brought into human communities at this time, fed and cared for, and selectively bred into dogs—the first animal domesticated by humans. The dogs became valuable hunting partners, watchdogs, and a source of food in hard times.

The hunter-gatherers also discovered fire and learned that cooked food was tastier, easier to digest, and more nutritious because it required less energy to metabolize. Cooking also killed harmful bacteria and microorganisms, and preserved meat for a short time. A glancing blow across a flint tool would produce a spark in a bed of dry leaves, and the resulting fire provided warmth on a cold night. It would be seen that a frozen carcass brought close to the fire would thaw and become edible, and the next step would have been to roast the meat over an open flame or boil it in its own skin, haggis-like, over hot stones. Boiling led to the preparation of soups and nutritious broths, which meant that the very young and the very old, whose teeth could not chew raw meat, were fed and cared for more effectively. Cooking not only made eating easier; it created the social ritual of the mealtime, when the family or clan group would gather around the cooking pit to engage the life-affirming act of eating and sharing.

The societies of hunter-gatherers are often thought of as rough and brutish, and their need to hunt seen as a fundamental source of human aggression. They were the first to develop killing weapons and certainly used them against other humans when they or their food sources were threatened. But by comparison with the later farming societies, the hunter-gatherers were peaceful and communal in their habits. They had little in the way of surpluses to fight over, and everyone's help was needed for hunting and cooking. The brutality of organized warfare and slavery does not appear as a major force in history until agriculture, with its ownership of land and its increased food supply, became a way of life.

Of course, the hunters were still also gatherers, and they continued to harvest the fruits and nuts and seeds of the forest, and they surely observed that many of the animals they hunted ate the wild grasses that spread across the plains and steppes. Their first attempts to imitate the animals were disappointing. The wild grazing animals of the grasslands had microorganisms in their stomachs that allowed them to convert plant tissue into animal protein. Humans have no such microorganisms in their digestive system and cannot obtain nourishment directly by eating grass. The nutritious seed heads of the grasses were edible, but pretty indigestible with their tough outer coatings of bran and chaff. But if the seeds were first boiled in water or crushed or ground in some way, the nutritious seed kernels could be sorted out by hand. Persistence solved the problem, and people were soon collecting these wild grasses and supplementing their diet with the nutritious seed heads.

After the Thaw

By about 13,000 years ago, the glaciers had fully receded and will remain in their present polar locations, we hope, for many thousands of years to come. Soon after the last great thaw, about 10,000 years ago, people in the warmer tropical and subtropical climates of the world began to experiment with the deliberate planting of the seeds they had gathered and stored, and they began to breed captured animals rather than killing them outright. The historian V. Gordon Childe called this transition to agriculture the Neolithic Revolution. Farming and animal breeding were new and revolutionary ways of producing food in sufficient abundance so that not everyone in the community was required to work all the time at acquiring food. This created time and labor that could be used for other activities. And people could be supported who produced no food at all. This was the starting point of civilization, when there was finally enough food to feed rulers, magicians, priests, full-time warriors, merchants, stonecutters, tanners, weavers, miners and metalworkers, servants and slaves, and all the other non-food-producing people in a modern, specialized, stratified society. But we are getting a little ahead of our story.

The little we know about the lives and eating habits of our prehistoric ancestors has been pieced together by paleontologists, archaeologists, and other scientists who study fossils and ancient human artifacts. In addition to the old skills of careful morphological analysis of bones and the plotting of digs, modern tools include sophisticated techniques such as radioactive carbon dating, accelerator mass spectrometry, scanning electron microscopy, and molecular biology. The scientific view changes and deepens every year with the discovery of each new prehistoric fragment, and, like all scientific visions, it becomes both clearer and more mysterious at the same time.

One may choose instead to believe that the Lord created the heavens and Earth and all the creatures upon it in six days, and rested on the seventh, and that He then planted a lush garden and provided the first man and woman with the fruits and seeds of all the plants of Earth in abundance. The man and woman then sinned by choosing to acquire their own knowledge of what was right and what was wrong, rather than follow the commandments of their creator. As punishment for their sin, they lost their immortality and were condemned to hard labor for the rest of their days in order to coax those food-bearing plants from a cursed and unyielding land.

This book cannot give much credit to pre-scientific accounts of human development, but we'll refer to these accounts from time to time because they speak worlds about the understanding of the human condition among the people who wrote them down. This particular Old Testament story of man's fall from divine grace, for example, speaks of the plants of the fields, and is clearly the work of chroniclers living in a settled agricultural society, far removed from the conditions faced by the first humans. It also speaks of labor as something difficult and painful, as something one would rather not do, as something which the first man and woman in the Garden of Eden knew nothing about. Most hunter-gatherer communities are in tune with their natural surroundings, and their members hunt, fish, cook, chop wood, and perform all the other necessary tasks of survival as and when they must, without a thought to the notion of work as an unpleasant concept. In fact, they have no abstract notion of "work" at all. But the idea of eating bread earned by the sweat of one's brow would have appealed to poor, hardworking farmers taxed by the ruler of some powerful city-state, and the myth reveals oppressive social relationships. It was, after all, written by people reflecting upon their deliverance from slavery. The idea of "work" only comes into being when there are people in human communities who don't work.

We turn now to the development of agriculture, a revolutionary new way of producing food, and to the ancient farming societies that recorded these myths of creation. The record of what happened now becomes richer and more complete, because it becomes a true historical, or written, record. Of all the non-food-producing people supported by the farmers, perhaps the most important was the scribe. Societies that produce abundant supplies of food need to keep track of their surpluses and how they are distributed, and how the land on which they are grown is divided up and used. The farmers needed accountants, and a system of arithmetic, and a symbolic form of language called writing, to keep a record of their affairs, and what was written down was difficult to dispute at a later time. There was a new power in the written word—it was to be believed, whether it recorded a business transaction, a law, or a myth. Written records accumulate, and writing gave the farmers a sense of their past, as well as expectations for the future. Even as they began to work in different ways, they became a community, a people, a nation. And civilization was born.

Chapter Two
The Development of Agriculture

Before the first seed could be placed in the ground, and indeed before plants themselves could take hold of the land in a big way, nature had to create a new material—the soil. Soil is a complicated substance, and part of that substance is alive. Soil contains not only a wide variety of minerals and chemicals, but also thousands of microorganisms and larger creatures that transform those inorganic materials into substances plants can use. Soil is also full of bits and pieces of dead things that living things can eat. Soil would not be soil without its bacteria and fungi and insects and the biochemical transformations they perform. The great English naturalist Charles Darwin once investigated the power of earthworms, through their excrement, to keep an English field fertile. The pores, or spaces between the particles of soil, trap atmospheric gases and water, which are vital to plants. It took millions of years of erosion and weathering before Earth's rock was broken down into tiny particles of sand and silt and clay, and millions of years more for evolution to add the living creatures that make soil the wonderful, mysterious, life-sustaining material that it is.

English naturalist Charles Darwin investigated how earthworms keep fields fertile.

As plant eaters, we are dependent on the soil and very fortunate to live on a planet where geological and evolutionary forces could create it. That said, we abuse the soil at our own peril. The soils of the Middle East and Saharan Africa once supported lush forests and grasslands, and they were also prime agricultural land. But, as the years have passed, erosion, endless warfare, and bad land management have turned much of these regions into desert. The great civilizations that once flourished there are now just empty cities buried in the infertile sand.

The development of agriculture, the discovery that a tiny seed placed in the ground would produce a living plant, has been described as a miracle. It certainly was miraculous in the way that it transformed the surface of the Earth and the human beings who lived upon it, but its discovery was the result not of miracle or accident, but of the kind of keen observation, wily intelligence, and persistent effort that is fired by hunger in the belly. From before the time that people were, well, people, our mammalian cousins the lemurs and tree shrews and their descendants—the Old World apes—lived an arboreal lifestyle high up in the forest canopy, and they hungered for the tastiness of its leaves and fruits, its nuts and seeds.

By the time the first ape-men and ape-women stood erect and left the dense forests to explore the open African grasslands, they must have had considerable knowledge of the food value of plants. They must have eaten new species experimentally as they moved along, carefully observing what other animals ate in order to avoid poisonous plants. As they watched and followed other predators onto the savanna, at first scavenging off the remains of kills and eventually learning to kill for themselves, they must have quickly realized that the herds of prehistoric antelope and gazelle and wildebeest they fed upon were themselves sustained by the wild grasses all around them. From the time that humans were humans, they must have had an intense interest in the growth of these wild grasses and the maturation of their seeds.

Grasses, Grains, and Seeds

The grasses, genus *Gramineae*, are angiosperms, plants that produce flowers and seeds in order to reproduce. Angiosperms comprise about 60 percent of all plant species and are the most widespread form of plant life on the surface of the Earth. There are more than 200,000 species of angiosperms, and about a dozen of these species are among the twenty or so plants that are of major importance to human beings as a source of food. Of these major food plants, the seed grains of the common grasses are the most important. The seeds of grasses used for food are also known as cereals, after Ceres, the Roman goddess of agriculture. Three species of grass—wheat, rice, and corn—feed the world.

The structure of cereal grains is complex. The seed is surrounded by an outer coating of bracts, also known as chaff, which is indigestible and must be removed before further processing. The seed itself may have a hard protective coating. The next layer consists of bran, which contains some carbohydrates, vitamins, and minerals. Underneath the bran is the endosperm, the food supply for the seed's embryo, which is rich is starch. Underneath the endosperm is the germ, the embryo itself, which contains proteins, fats, starch, and vitamins and minerals. As tiny as these seed grains are, they are produced in great abundance, are relatively easy to gather, and when their moisture content is reduced by drying, they can be stored for relatively long periods of time without spoiling.

The hunter-gatherer communities collected and ate these grasses long before they understood how to grow them. But the desire to increase the available food supply, to reduce the uncertainty of survival, was a powerful factor in motivating people to learn more about valued plants and how to "encourage" their abundance. The nomadic hunters must have noted how the migratory routes of the herds followed the lushest grasslands, and how those lush areas were associated with certain kinds of land and climate. They must have noted how the plants matured with the seasons, and when was the best time to gather the nutritious seed heads. They would have

Ceres, the Roman goddess of agriculture. The word cereal *is derived from her name.*

learned that if they came upon a stand of mature grass too late in the season, the coveted seeds would have broken off the plants and been carried away by the wind. They must have learned which seeds tasted best and which were not yet ripe. They learned that the seeds, if kept dry and protected from rot, could be stored and carried along with them, to be eaten at a later time. And as they stored and handled seeds and carried them from one place to another, they would have discovered that if some of the seeds were dropped on the ground, there would be new stands of grass when they returned next season to the place where the seeds were discarded.

Eventually the hunter-gatherers learned to associate seeds with the appearance of new plant life, though their understanding of plant reproduction was cast in purely magical terms. Still, the discovery must have excited their practical imagination. Primitive patterns of plant "management" began to emerge. Seeds might be "broadcast" or scattered across the ground wherever people hoped to expand their food supply, and the success or failure of these first experiments in deliberate planting taught people a great deal about the hardiness of different plants under varying ecological conditions, and the types of soil and moisture conditions that best suited those plants. Efforts were made to keep the wild herds from grazing on the patches of wild food plants, and competing plants were cleared or burned away to give the precious food plants more room. A little experimentation would have shown that seeds pushed into the ground were harder for birds and insects to get at and could better survive harsh winters.

The Primitive Landscape

The landscape that the hunter-gatherers passed through began to change its appearance in subtle ways as the more desirable plants extended their range, with human assistance. It was increasingly a managed rather than a wild landscape along the routes that people traveled. Wherever the hunter-gatherers lingered, the bush and the forest were pushed back, and the wild grasses flourished. As more was learned about the conditions that made the grasses grow, more time had to be spent managing them. Though life was still nomadic and the greatest efforts were still devoted to the hunt, the notion of "tending" the land had arisen. There was now an incentive, if not yet to settle in one place, to at least confine migrations to regular routes and frequently revisit those areas where human efforts had increased the stock of edible plant life. It was, after all, necessary to be camped near the food plants when they ripened and to gather them quickly before the seeds dispersed in the wind.

This primitive gathering of wild grasses and other plants went on for tens of thousands of years in human prehistory as small bands of people spread out from Africa across the continents, discovering the lush vegetation of the world's river valleys and floodplains and grasslands and marshes. But all this activity still involved only the gathering of wild plants, of taking what nature provided rather than changing nature. The key to true agriculture, the process of *domestication*, of creating new species of plants and animals for human use, did not begin until between 10,000 and 5,000 years ago, developing independently in several different regions of the world—the Near East, Central and South America, eastern China, sub-Saharan Africa, and, scientists have recently concluded, eastern North America.

Scientists have a fairly clear picture of when agriculture was developed in these different regions and what plants were chosen for domestication, principally through the physical examination and radioactive carbon dating of seeds found in ancient settlements. But the question of *why* human beings gave up hunting and turned to agriculture remains a mystery. The obvious answer, to produce more food, is not so obvious. If the early hunter-gatherer communities could find an abundance of game animals to feed themselves, there would have been no incentive to control the lifecycle of the grasses and increase their supply. If game animals were not abundant and the food supply was uncertain, hunting and gathering would have required more effort, and it seems unlikely that people would have had the time to put seeds in the ground and wait for them to grow. Many ingenious explanations have been put forward to account for the origins of farming.

Climate and population pressure probably had something to do with the agricultural revolution. Though the ice sheets had receded, the cold had forced human communities into a relatively narrow band of tropical and subtropical areas, roughly the same areas that were first farmed. These areas were extensively settled by different human groups, and it may not have been possible for hunter-gatherers to range so freely in their search for food animals without coming into conflict with others. Another factor was water. Many of the first farming settlements were located near regions richly watered by rivers, streams, lakes, and marshes. These waters provided abundant fish and waterfowl that enabled settled groups to stay in one place much of the time, giving them the leisure to experiment with planting.

Rituals and Religion

Primitive religion may also have played its part. Early humans felt a mystical kinship toward the animals they hunted and performed rituals designed to appease the gods who provided these sources of food. After a successful hunt, some animals were not eaten, but sacrificed to these gods. As religious rituals became more substantial, sacrificial animals would have to be kept and cared for until the time of the sacrifice, and perhaps this was the incentive to domesticate them. The same was true of plants. After the gathering of the wild grasses, a portion of the seeds were scattered on the ground and "returned" to the earth goddess as an offering to ensure more plants next season. In ancient times, when someone was buried, many of that person's possessions, including perhaps a pouch of seeds, were buried with the person to ensure survival in the next life. People would have observed how plants flourished in the disturbed soil of grave sites near their settlements. In 1897, Canadian novelist and philosopher Grant Allen suggested that primitive peoples would have thought that the spirit of the dead

Early humans felt they had to please the gods through the offering of animal sacrifices.

person could somehow ensure the fertility of the earth, and that this idea led to the practice of human sacrifice.

The relationship among human sacrifice, the fertility of the land, and the shaping of the first agricultural societies was explored by the Scottish anthropologist Sir James George Frazer in his classic book, *The Golden*

Bough, published in 1890. Frazer suggested that leaders of these societies, at first headmen and shamans, and later kings and priests, were thought to have magical powers and were charged with ensuring the bounty of the harvest. When the harvests failed, or the leaders were felt to be losing their powers, they were killed and replaced by new leaders with more vigorous powers. This, of course, was hard on the rulers, who in time were able to perpetuate their rule by designating scapegoats, other human beings or animals, in place of themselves for the ritual sacrifice. But the notion of the death and resurrection of the god-king was linked in ancient mythology to the success of agricultural activity. When the hunter-gatherers began to bury their dead, they were likely to see a magical connection between their own deaths and the regeneration of food plants, what Betty Fussell in *The Story of Corn* called "the interchange of blood with sap and flesh with grain."[1] And out of this came one of the great, ancient religious mysteries connecting death to the fertility of the earth and the renewal of life.

Early Settlements

At any rate, within certain subtropical geographical regions, great success was achieved in fostering the growth of wild grasses as food plants. Specific localities where the grasses were abundant became important enough to maintain and guard all year round, and the first permanent settlements began to appear even while hunting remained vital. People soon discovered that it was possible to stop moving around and still eat. In the 1970s, botanist Jack R. Harlan of the University of Illinois, gathering wild wheat by hand with a flint sickle in southeastern Turkey, was able to collect 4 pounds (1.8 kg) of grain an hour, proving that a farm family could collect enough grain in three weeks to feed themselves for the entire year. As yields increased, so did human numbers. As more seeds were collected than could be immediately eaten, and as it was recognized that some of these seeds should not be eaten but set aside for growing more grasses, storage became a problem. The solution was a hot fire and plenty of mud. Fire dried the seeds for storage and baked the mud into clay. Clay urns and jars replaced containers made from animal skins or woven from plant fibers. Hot fires, mud, and dead grass could also be used to make bricks for more permanent dwellings. The plant gatherers also made crude wood and bone sickles and digging sticks for planting and harvesting, and stone choppers and grinding slabs to make the seeds edible. The sedentary lifestyle and the growing dependence on the wild grasses for food produced a higher level of material culture. The first divisions of wealth appeared as some families and communities prospered through their efforts and others did not.

In the process of establishing more permanent settlements and extending the growth of the wild grasses, people tended to open up the land, to clear away the unwanted undergrowth from their living areas and make sure that the edible plants were well separated from the encroaching wild vegetation. Soon it became clear that planting seeds in isolated plots made the grasses easier to protect and manage. Isolating these plants from their wild neighbors was a critical step in the process of domestication. When the seeds of grasses are gathered in the wild, it is the remaining *uncollected* seeds that produce the next generation of plants, and of course these seeds simply produce more wild plants. But when a plot of wild grass is grown and harvested in isolation, interesting things happen. Now it is the *collected* seeds that produce the next generation of plants. How human beings choose those seeds determines the genetic characteristics of the next crop. These first farmers gathered seeds selectively and replanted only those seeds that they thought would produce superior food plants. Over time, these isolated plots began to yield a kind of grass that was distinctly different from its wild neighbors.

Changing the Plants

Plants, of course, had been adapting to environmental change for millions of years through the process of natural selection, but the plants had a different agenda from their consumers. The wild grasses thrived best with small, light seeds with thick, hard coatings that could be borne on the wind or dispersed after being eaten by birds or small mammals. Sometimes it was important to put growth energy into sturdy stalks tall enough to outreach other plants in the competition for sunlight. More energy might be expended in synthesizing biochemicals for protection against fungal infections and insect predators. Plants in the wild have many demands on their energy resources, and designing big, nutritious, easily picked seeds for human beings isn't one of them. Furthermore, plants that vary in size, rates of growth, and response to climatic extremes are the best survivors in the wild, though these qualities also make them difficult for people to manage.

Wild plants adapt according to their own needs, but in these first, small isolated plots, humans had intervened in the life cycle of the wild grasses and established new conditions for their evolutionary success. The seeds of grasses with "wild" qualities were not collected for replanting, and the seeds of the chosen plants passed on the qualities that humans preferred. These primitive agriculturists naturally harvested the seeds that were larger in size and therefore more nutritious. They selected seeds with thinner outer coatings, because the hard coatings were a hindrance to grinding and digesting the seeds. They looked for grasses that grew rapidly in dense stands and displayed their seeds in a compact cluster at the top of the plant, which made gathering easier. They preferred plants that matured together and ripened at the same time, and they wanted seed clusters that were strong enough not to disperse in the wind before they were collected. They made these choices out of immediate need, and had no idea of how genetic inheritance worked, but the selection process did its work all the same. Not only were certain species of wild grasses thus chosen over others for human consumption, but the chosen plants themselves were changed by this long and painstaking process of artificial selection.

The plants adapted to the needs of their human masters and evolved into new species, and in some cases completely lost their ability to survive in the wild. *Zea mays*, for example, the modern corn plant, is a descendant of the Central American wild grass known as teosinte, but it has been so altered by human efforts that its seed pod is enclosed in a leafy husk and is too firmly attached to the plant to disperse in the wind. Corn cannot survive unless people replant it. But these domesticated species had greater food value and were easier to harvest. Domesticated plants are new species that have given up much of the hardiness needed to survive in the wild in favor of the large compacted seed pods and regimented growth characteristics that people wanted. The new plants had become, in a manner of speaking, fat and lazy—qualities also much desired in the animals that people were learning to domesticate. Such plants no longer had the natural defenses or the genetic diversity to thrive under harsh ecological pressures, and they depended upon human cultivators to provide nurturing and protection. Without human care, the preferred plants would die off, and the surviving plants would revert to their wild characteristics.

Early Farming

The first deliberate efforts to farm occurred between 10,000 and 8,000 years ago in the Near East in an area known as the Fertile Crescent, the site of present-day Iraq, Iran, Turkey, Syria, Lebanon, Israel, and Jordan. Here the Saudi Arabian desert pushes up into the mountain forests of Kurdistan, creating a 1,500-mile (2,400-km) crescent-shaped region of fertile grasslands and woodlands. It is bordered in the east by the lush valleys of the Tigris and Euphrates Rivers and in the west by smaller rivers and lakes along the Mediterranean coast. Here, 10,000 years ago, the hunter-gatherers flourished by preying upon the herds of deer and gazelle, the flocks of wildfowl, the wild ancestors of sheep, goats, and pigs, and by hunting the aurochs, the huge and ornery wild ancestors of cattle. But they also gathered wild fruits and nuts, legumes, flax, and the seeds of many wild grasses, especially the seeds of wild barley and emmer and einkorn wheat.

The beginnings of real farming began in an area called the Fertile Crescent.

Wheat, genus *Triticum*, was an excellent choice. It is a highly adaptable grass, able to grow in a wide variety of soils and climates, and it thrives in either cold or hot, dry conditions. It produces a good yield of seeds, with a protein content that varies from 7 percent to almost 15 percent, and it is rich in the B vitamins—thiamin, riboflavin, and niacin. The seeds can be easily dried and stored.

Unlike other cereal grains, when mixed with water the proteins in wheat form gluten, a sticky, elastic substance that is the basis of dough, from which people can make light and nutritious loaves of bread. The hunter-gatherers did not make bread, but by removing the chaff, grinding the seeds, and mixing them with water, a nutritious gruel could be prepared. If yeast infected the gruel, the result was a nutritious form of beer, though today barley is the preferred grain for making beer malt. If the grains were roasted over a fire, they would keep indefinitely.

The wild wheat and barley grew naturally on the well-drained slopes of higher elevations. The people transported them to the well-watered lowlands, and the plants proved adaptable to the new climate. These grasses grew in thick stands that made harvesting convenient. Selecting only the best seeds for replanting, the people over time genetically altered these wild species and domesticated them. Early barley had only two rows of seeds in its seed pack, but, by about 9,000 years ago, people were growing a new species of barley with six rows of seeds, giving the plant three times the food value of the wild variety. Wheat was also transformed. Each seed of wheat consists of a seed kernel with one or more spikelets—long, arrow-shaped tubes that help the seed penetrate and embed itself in the soil. The seed itself is attached to the plant by a small stem called a rachis. In wild wheat, the rachis is very brittle, so that the seed pod can shatter, or break off easily from the plant and be carried away by the wind. This would cause havoc during the harvest as the grain scattered before people could gather it in, so these first farmers collected for replanting only the seeds whose rachis stayed attached to the plant. After many replantings, their fields were full of a new kind of wheat with a tougher rachis. This wheat was easier for human beings to collect, though with seeds that were reluctant to separate from the plant, it would have had a very tough time surviving back in the wild.

The Beginnings of Animal Breeding

The people of the Fertile Crescent also learned that it was easier to capture and breed wild animals than to hunt them. Young animals might be captured after their parents were killed in the hunt, brought back to settlements and kept as pets, and some magical but workable understanding of how they bred was acquired. Wild sheep, goats, pigs, and aurochs were rounded up and grazed on nearby slopes or fed the straw and stubble left over from the harvests, and their manure helped to fertilize the fields. The animals changed too. People looked for species that were docile, prone to submissive group behavior, less able to run away, simple to feed, and accepting of their new human masters. They often took the larger animals and the aggressive males out of their herds or castrated them to calm their behavior. As a result, domesticated animals became smaller and more manageable than their wild ancestors. The herds generally consisted of many females and young animals, with only a few males for breeding—a gender and age composition that would not normally have been found in nature. The ancient wild auroch, for example, was a huge and unsociable beast with long horns and shoulders that stood as high as a man's head, and it was dangerous to hunt. But the auroch is now extinct. In its place, humans created modern cattle that will spend all day dumbly grazing with no thought of wandering off and at the end of the day can be rounded up by a small boy and his dog.

The animals domesticated by human beings include some oddities, like the silk moth and the honey bee, but it was the *Artiodactyla*, or hoofed animals, that turned out to be the most useful species. These animals are called ruminants. They all have the capacity to eat grasses and turn plant protein into animal protein, something humans cannot do, and they provided food for people where none existed before. Domesticated sheep came from the wild mouflon, which grazed on mountain slopes at higher elevations where cooler temperatures prevailed. But its breathing mechanism allowed the animal to dissipate body heat, and in spite of its thick coat of wool it proved adaptable to the warmer climate of the lowlands, where people preferred to live. The goat is descended from the wild bezoar and provided a milk that is similar to human milk. Though no longer an important source of meat today, one variety, the Angora goat, provides us with a valuable wool called mohair.

Cattle, of course, were humankind's greatest achievement in animal husbandry. They provided high-protein meat and leather for clothing, as they always had for the hunter-gatherers, but under domestication they also provided milk and cheese, power to pull loads, and dung, which made the grasses grow more vigorously and could also be burned for fuel. Today there are many varieties of cattle throughout the world, individually bred for superior meat or milk production, and beefsteak is considered one of the world's finest foods. But these first domesticated cattle were thin and scrawny, and what meat they did have was fairly tough. The animals were mostly valuable for their milk, their manure, and their ability to pull. There is a misconception about how much meat people ate after the domestication of cattle. Meat was not a common part of people's diets, though they ate enough to provide themselves with the proteins unavailable from plants. But it took a lot of grain to feed cattle. They were expensive to raise and too valuable to slaughter if other foods were available. Because of this, beef would eventually become a luxury food for the rich and was rarely found on the farmer's table.

Wherever these early agriculturists could practice both farming and animal husbandry, they found that their permanent settlements were quite self-sufficient. The remains of the harvest fed the animals, and the animals manured the fields and kept them fertile. Large animals like oxen could be used to trample the grain so that the chaff could be picked out, and they could also be used to pull the simple plows that people were now using to put seeds into the ground. By about 6,000 B.C., throughout the Fertile Crescent the economies of many small villages and permanent settlements, as well as a number of larger communities resembling small walled cities with even higher levels of social organization, were based on different combinations of farming and animal husbandry. In some areas, the people depended almost exclusively on farming; in other areas, herding prevailed; and in still other areas, a more modern system of mixed farming and livestock-raising was the norm.

Groups based on different ways of life developed different religious practices and cultural values, as well as different attitudes toward how the land was used, how water was shared, and how wealth and status were parceled out within their communities. People who depended exclusively on herding remained semi-nomadic, taking their animals back and forth between the cool mountain pastures in the summer and the warmer lowlands in the winter. They needed open land and free access to water, and constant movement across the empty grasslands kept their culture simple. Farmers needed to enclose the land, assign caretakers to the different plots, and regulate water usage. Farming required disciplined activity, and farmers calculated the value of their labor by the size of the harvests.

Cultural Conflict

The result was serious friction between some of these groups. The Old Testament tell us that Adam's son Abel was a keeper of sheep, and his son Cain was a tiller of the ground. The ancient Israelites were nomadic pastoralists, herders of sheep and goats, and the austere environment of the mountains and the desert had given them simple egalitarian values and a strong sense of brotherhood. They looked upon the Amorites, their neighbors in the land of Caanan, with suspicion, because the Amorites farmed and lived in larger settled communities with class divisions, land ownership, and great disparities of wealth between rich and poor. So the ancient Hebrews had their god favor Abel, the herder, over his brother Cain, the farmer, and when Cain sought revenge upon his brother by killing him, the

After killing Abel, who was a herder, Cain, who was a farmer, was cursed by the Hebrew God.

god of the Hebrews cursed the farmer and sent him away. These frictions may also have been responsible for the Jewish prohibition against the eating of pork. It is unlikely that ancient people understood the cause of trichinosis or the dangers of eating undercooked pork. The pig, however, though a sociable animal, is notoriously difficult to herd. It is a scavenger rather than a grazer, and is content to dig for refuse in the disturbed soils around human settlements. The nomadic Hebrews associated the pig with the settled farming communities of their enemies. Later, of course, when the Jews established their own kingdoms in the region—based upon a farming economy and replete with all the same divisions of wealth and status—their god made peace with agriculture. But the old message of the desert was still heard in the fiery speeches of the prophets, who railed against the injustices of their newly stratified society.

The new value given to the land and the food security it could create made farmers the envy of others, and with agriculture we see the beginning of organized warfare. With an agricultural surplus, human numbers began to increase. It was now possible to feed full-time soldiers, as well as the miners and metalworkers who made their bronze and iron weapons, and the slaves who would be captured in battle. Land was now worth fighting for. One animal figured prominently in the history of these ancient conflicts between pastoral herders and tillers of the land. Though it had little food value, or rather, was too valuable to use for food, it gave the herders a tremendous advantage over the tillers. Descended from the wild tarpan and domesticated about 5,000 years ago, bred for size, strength, endurance, agility, intelligence, and obedience, the horse became a weapon of war and conquest.

For a long time to come, the mounted riders of nomadic peoples and the chariot-drawn armies of conquerors terrorized the tillers of the land. From the time of the Fertile Crescent's first agricultural empires until the Middle Ages, the horse elevated the warrior above the farmer and the nobleman above the peasant, helping to push the tillers to the bottom of the social hierarchy, where they have remained ever since. The tillers were tied to their land, whereas the horsemen could roam freely and live off the harvests as predators. By the time of the Middle Ages, the mounted warrior was considered a nobleman, someone who was born superior to a tiller, who owned the lands the tiller worked on, and who had a divine right to benefit from the tiller's labor. Mounted on a huge and powerful horse, encased in armor, swinging a mace or a battle-ax and charging forward at a gallop, the medieval knight was the equivalent of a fourteenth-century tank, and no poorly equipped peasant army could stand against him.

The tillers did not get their revenge until the fourteenth and fifteenth centuries, when the English kings discovered a lethal new weapon—the Welsh longbow—and forced their tillers to practice with it in their time away from the fields. With this powerful and accurate bow and arrow, the tillers no longer had to rush and grapple with the knights on their horses. They could kill them at a distance. The peasant soldier, who lacked the wealth to own a horse and equip himself with armor, now only needed a keen eye and a strong arm—farm skills—to fight the knights. At the Battles of Crecy in 1346 and Agincourt in 1415, English armies with battalions of archers slaughtered the mounted knights and changed forever the relationship between the mounted noblemen and the tillers. If an army could be recruited from a mass of men with little wealth or battle skill or horsemanship, there was little reason for the nobleman to exist, or to claim the allegiance and the crops of the tillers.

In ancient times, the intermixing of these different economies, of farmers and pastoralists, was healthy. It gave the people of the Fertile Crescent a variety of strategies for food production that could be fine-tuned to different environments. This was one of the reasons why the agricultural revolution spread rapidly out of the Fertile Crescent. By about 7,000 years ago, well-developed farming communities flourished in Greece, Italy, and in other areas of southern Europe along the Mediterranean coast. By about 6,000 years ago, the people of northern Europe had figured out how to adjust the growth cycle of wheat and barley to their cooler climate and shorter growing seasons, and farming villages had spread to northern France and Germany and Russia.

Grain and Empire

At about the same time, the revolution also spread south, into northeastern Africa and the valley of the Nile, where the fertile floodplains of that immense river yielded rich harvests of wheat. At its origin in Equatorial Africa, tropical rains carried silt and vegetable matter into the Nile, and the nutrient-rich waters poured into the lowlands in a yearly flood sometime between July and September. When the Nile floods, it normally drains into the Mediterranean rather quickly, leaving only a narrow band of fertile land between the encroaching desert. By channeling and diverting some of the floodwaters, however, the ancient Egyptians were able to extend the floodwaters over a wider area of land, vastly increasing the area suitable for planting. This required the cooperation of thousands of farmers all along the length of the river, all working to a master plan, and all coordinating their actions on the basis of shared information about what was happening elsewhere.

Irrigation projects on this scale meant "big government" and a disciplined, obedient peasantry willing to pay taxes for its administration. A unified empire appeared along the Nile around 3,000 B.C., and it remained relatively stable for thousands of years, so important was the river to its prosperity. The Egyptian pharaoh was worshiped as the son of the gods and was deified upon his death. He owned all the land and with the help of his priests he organized the labor for the channeling of the waters. Each year, after the floodwaters receded, the farmers harnessed their primitive wooden plows to their oxen and prepared the fields for planting. The principal crops were wheat and barley, and for the most part the Egyptians subsisted on coarse breads, grain porridges, and fermented beers, but in their gardens they grew onions, cucumbers, beans, radishes, scallions, date palms, and wine grapes. They also raised cattle, sheep, goats, ducks, and geese. Between planting and harvesting, there was time and food to engage in vast construction projects—new canals, palaces, temples, and tombs. So fertile was the mud of the Nile Valley, and so favorable was the climate, that crops could be grown all year round. Egypt became the granary of the entire Mediterranean region, and up until the time of Christ, invading armies would try to control the wealth of its harvests.

New Kingdoms

In the area of the Tigris and Euphrates Rivers, known as ancient Mesopotamia, there was more natural rainfall and less dependence on a central authority to control the floodwaters. Here, from 3,000 B.C. to 600 B.C., a series of smaller and less stable kingdoms flowered and were then consumed by endless warfare. The Sumerians were replaced by the Babylonians, who were replaced by the Assyrians, who were replaced by the Chaldeans, who were replaced by the Persians. These wars of conquest were waged with utter ruthlessness, and the enemy's agricultural base was not ignored. After he had recaptured the rebellious city of Babylon in 689 B.C., Sennacherib of Assyria reported, "I leveled the city and its houses from the foundations to the top. I destroyed them and consumed them with fire. I tore down and removed the outer and inner walls, the temples and the ziggurats built of brick, and dumped the rubble in the Arahtu Canal. And after I had destroyed Babylon, smashed its gods and massacred its population, I tore up its soil and threw it into the Euphrates so that it was carried by the river down to the sea."[2] Continuous warfare was one of the major causes of environmental degradation and the ultimate decline in agricultural productivity in this region.

Meanwhile, agriculture was also discovered in the Sahel, a region of tropical east Africa that lies south of the Sahara desert within the modern nations of Mauritania, Mali, Niger, Senegal, Upper Volta, and the countries along the Gulf of Guinea. Between the desert and the tropical rain forest to the south, a broad band of rolling grasslands was subject to a rainy season that created many small lakes and marshes. Here, between 5,000 and 3,000 years ago, the east Africans began to domesticate wild cattle and three new wild grasses: millet, sorghum, and African rice. Both farming and herding communities appeared, and complex economic relationships developed between them. The pastoralists provided the farmers with meat, milk, dung, and the pulling power of their animals in exchange for grain and water rights, and the region proved prosperous enough to support several kingdoms.

Agriculture in China

About 8,000 years ago, half a world away in east Asia, the Chinese also developed agriculture. From their origin on the Tibetan Plateau, two great rivers flow east to the sea across 1,000 miles (1,600 km) of fertile land—the Huang Ho, or Yellow River, in the north, and the Yangtze River in the south. The Yangtze flows southeast then east through a region blessed with a mild and warm climate. Parts of southern China enjoy subtropical weather. Here the first Neolithic farmers discovered and domesticated a new wild grass, *Oryza sativa*, or rice. Wild rice grew in the lowland river deltas in the coastal regions of China, and it sometimes spread inland along the river valleys where there was regular seasonal flooding. Unlike other grasses, rice had developed a complicated lifecycle tied to the ebb and flow of the river. Its seeds are dispersed by the floodwaters and lodge in the ground when the waters recede. There they lie dormant until the next flood, when they germinate and grow underwater. Along the entire length of the Yangtze Valley, the wild rice took hold in extensive areas of shallow freshwater lakes and marshes. People took this wild rice and replanted it near their upland settlements, where the worst of the flooding could be avoided or controlled. To provide the shallow beds of water that the rice needed to grow, they used

Nearly 8,000 years ago, China began growing rice in flooded rice paddies.

a system of mud dikes and mountainside terraces to enclose the water in rain-fed paddies.

The rice was threshed by spreading the grains on the ground and having animals trample them to break the chaff off the seeds. The lighter chaff was then winnowed out by tossing the grain in the air and letting the wind carry it off. Then the rice was ground to remove the hulls, the inner protective seed coatings, which produces brown rice. If the layer of bran is then removed, white rice is produced. Brown rice with the bran intact is more nutritious than white rice, but it takes longer to cook and contains oils that will cause the rice to spoil if stored for a long time. There are two broad categories of rice: short-grained *japonica*, which produces sticky rice when cooked, and long-grain *indica*, which is the dominant variety grown in Asia, though it has a lower yield than *japonica*.

This system of flooded rice paddies and terraced slopes presented some interesting problems. The nature of the terrain worked against the development of advanced, mechanical methods of harvesting, and even today much rice is planted and gathered by labor-intensive methods, usually by women. And rice, especially white rice, has a very low protein and vitamin content, so those who depend upon it exclusively often suffer from malnutrition or vitamin deficiency diseases such as beriberi. But the flooded fields could also be used for raising fish, a good source of protein, and the fish ate the larvae of mosquitoes and other insects that plagued farmers. So, to improve their diets, the Chinese domesticated the carp and raised them in the paddies.

Among the animals domesticated in southern China were the water buffalo, the pig, and the chicken. The water buffalo likes to wallow in rivers and streams and eat the aquatic grasses in the riverbed. It was an ideal animal for work in the flooded rice paddies, though it was too valuable to slaughter for meat. The pig, being a scavenger, was relatively cheap to raise, because it could be fed with human refuse or silage—the chopped-up, unused portion of the harvested crops. Unfortunately, pigs are susceptible to many diseases that can be transmitted to humans. Many influenza epidemics originate in China and are believed to be caused by the way pigs are raised by farmers there. The chicken, descended from a wild, flightless jungle fowl, has become one of the most important food animals in the world, valued for its eggs as well as its meat. It is more efficient than the pig in converting its feed into animal protein, and it requires little space to raise.

Wet rice farming also spread southward into the Indus River Valley in

Northwestern India and into Southeast Asia, where the warm tropical climate encouraged farmers to domesticate many other wild plants: sugar cane; the banana; root crops such as the taro, arrowroot, and yam; citrus fruits such as the orange, lemon, and grapefruit, as well as the coconut and the breadfruit; and spices such as clove, nutmeg, and pepper. Sugar cane is a tall grass whose stem yields a sweet juice that can be boiled into pure crystals of sugar, providing a source of quick energy and a sweetener for other foods. The banana grows on a tall leafy stalk that looks like a tree but isn't, and the fruit is actually classified as a berry. It was probably domesticated in Malaysia, reached Africa about 2,000 years ago, and was widely cultivated in tropical America by A.D. 1600. The yam never became a major food plant outside the tropics, but it had a major impact on global hunger in an indirect way by helping to control population. Chemicals originally derived from the yam were used to synthesize the first oral contraceptive in the 1950s. The coconut, a member of the palm family, is a rich source of both carbohydrates and protein. Its fruit can float in seawater for more than three months, and this quality, as well as the journeys of ancient Polynesian seafarers, helped to spread the coconut throughout Southeast Asia and the Pacific islands.

In northern China, along the valley of the Huang Ho River, the climate was colder and the rains were less dependable. Here, farmers domesticated millet, a new species of grass that was more resistant to drought. By about 6,500 years ago, there were fairly large farming settlements all along the Huang Ho. But they enjoyed an uneasy relationship with the fierce herders of horses and yaks who lived on the rolling grasslands to the north. Here, as in the Fertile Crescent, the need to manage the floodwaters and the threat of invasion from the north produced a strong, centralized government. There were more than 1,000 small kingdoms in China during the "Era of Contending (or Warring) States," until the Emperor Chin Shih Huang in 221 B.C. took possession of the eastern lowlands surrounding both of the great river valleys and founded the first Chinese empire. The emperors were the sons of heaven, but they could lose the blessing of heaven if floods, drought, or crop failure brought disaster, which it frequently did. The Chinese claim the oldest continuous civilization in the world, with 3,500 years of recorded history, but that history was replete with civil wars, peasant rebellions, and dynastic revolutions.

China's Turmoil

The reason for this turmoil was the particularly troublesome system of land ownership that arose in China. The frequent floods, droughts, and other natural disasters played havoc with the small farmers and drove many of them into debt to the larger, wealthier farmers. Many had to sell their farms and become tenants on other people's land. Over time, above the peasantry, a large class of parasitic landlords arose to manage the agricultural system and collect taxes for the emperor. Supposedly, imperial civil servants were selected through civil service examinations, but only the landlords could afford to educate their sons. So in addition to owning the land, they became a class of scholar-aristocrats, known as mandarins, upon whom the emperor depended for administering government affairs. The emperor was usually isolated in the capital, and across the country the mandarin landlords treated the peasantry with indifference , often refusing to open up their private granaries when the crops failed. The Chinese system is often called feudal, but it differed from medieval European feudalism in one important way. The peasants were not tied to the land by custom, and the landlords had no obligation to feed them in hard times. If the Chinese peasant could not pay his rent or taxes or debts, he was free to wander off and starve, while the landlord assigned his land to someone else. This oppressive system was sustained by the philosophy of Confucianism, which preached the obedience of son to father, of peasant to landlord, and of all to the emperor. The catch, however, was that the emperor, like the rulers of other agricultural empires, was responsible for the prosperity of the nation, and famine and hard times meant that the emperor had lost the blessing of heaven. This was justification for revolution, but in the absence of a more democratic political philosophy, China's peasant rebellions and civil wars degenerated into dynastic struggles. The only result was the installation of a new emperor and the continuation of the oppressive system.

China actually has very little arable land, considering its size and its enormous population. The rice fields had to be cultivated carefully and intensively, and except for a few chickens, pigs, and the water buffalo, there was no grain to spare for other types of livestock. Meat was rare even in the diets of the wealthy. This had unfortunate consequences during the Mongol invasion of the thirteenth century, because the Chinese armies had no grain to maintain horses for battle. The Mongols had horses, as well as accurate bows and arrows, and their swift-moving cavalry easily conquered China.

Agriculture in the New World

Agriculture was also developed independently in the New World. Between 20,000 and 15,000 years ago, when the Pleistocene glaciers had converted the ocean waters into ice sheets and sea levels were much lower, a land bridge was uncovered across the Bering Strait, and hunter-gatherers from Asia crossed over into North America. Searching for a more moderate climate, they moved south, and by about 12,000 years ago, human communities had spread all the way into South America. By about 5,000 years ago, we see the first evidence of the domestication of plants and animals in the central highlands of Mexico, where numerous small rivers flow out of the mountains into the Pacific. Here people learned to grow beans, peas, potatoes, squash, peppers, avocado, guava, peanuts, and what would become the most important food crop in the Americas: maize, or corn.

The story of corn reveals the power of human beings to selectively breed plants to increase their food value. Maize is a descendant of the wild grass teosinte, which still grows in Mexico today. The first maize plants had very small seed heads, or cobs, no more than 1 or 2 inches (2.5 to 5 cm) long, with only eight rows of six to nine kernels each. The tiny cobs grew on many small stalks and were difficult to gather. After centuries of selective harvesting, the cobs grew larger and developed more rows of kernels, and the cobs themselves began to grow along one sturdy, central stalk, which made collecting them easier. By about A.D. 1500, the farmers of Central America had produced a cob six times larger than the first domesticated maize plants. Though it was not until modern times and the invasion of the Europeans that corn came to resemble the plant we know today, the farmers of Central and South America had developed a nutritious food plant that would eventually produce the surpluses needed to build up an extensive civilization.

There are many different varieties of corn, in part because people have been experimenting with the plant for so long. Today, dent corn is the variety most widely grown for livestock feed, and sweet corn is the variety that most people eat. But the first corn grown by the farmers of Central America had a hard seed coating and had to be heated until it burst before it could be eaten, making popcorn the first variety gathered and planted. Corn could also be ground into meal for bread and tortillas, or it could be fermented into a beer known as chicha. Early beers of this type had a low alcohol content and were thick with grain. They were a kind of liquid bread and were consumed in great quantities by the poorer classes.

Though there was no great river valley in Central America, here again the need to organize the planting of the corn produced centralized autocratic societies with god-kings who held absolute power over their subjects. In Central and South America, the Aztec, the Inca, and the Maya absorbed or enslaved surrounding groups and established great kingdoms based on corn. The land was divided into separate areas—one portion for the farmers, another for the king, and a third portion for the sun-god, which really belonged to the priests. The tillers built canals and dikes and terraced the steep slopes with masonry walls to hold water. They fertilized the fields with human excrement, guano from the flocks of seabirds along the Pacific coast, and the uneaten parts of sardines. Kernels of corn were the principal form of currency, and images of corn appear over and over again in their works of art. The theme of death and resurrection was central to their religions. Human beings were sacrificed to keep the land fertile, and in ritual offerings, the kings sprinkled the fields with their own blood.

Farming soon spread out of Mexico throughout Central America, into northern South America, and south across the Andes mountains of Ecuador and Peru. Corn does not grow well at high elevations, and people in the high Andes domesticated other plants such as quinoa, a brightly colored grass favored by grazing animals, and the potato. The potato is a tuber, a big food sack attached to the underground root of the plant, from which a new plant will grow in a process known as vegetative reproduction, without either flowering or dispersing seed. Growing underground, the potato could survive the cold mountain frosts, and being rich in starch, it became a staple food of the highland farmers.

The people of the Andes also began to herd and breed the local mountain grazers for their meat, milk, and strength as pack animals. Two such animals, both related, oddly, to the camel family, were tamed—the wild guanaco was bred to become the llama, and the wild vicuña became the alpaca. The wool from the vicuña and the alpaca, considered the world's finest, made warm clothing for the cold mountain nights. People also carried their agricultural techniques from the western highlands into the tropical rain forests to the east, where they learned to cultivate other root crops such as manioc. Manioc, also called cassava or yuca, is not widely known outside the tropics, though tapioca pudding is made from it. It grew well in the poor soils and moist climate of the jungle. All that was required was to slash and burn a small clearing and stick a slice of the stem into the ground. The result was a very tall plant with an underground tuber that was rich in carbohydrates.

From its roots in Central America, the planting of maize, beans, and squash also spread north into the southwestern regions of the United States by about 3,000 years ago and had reached the eastern woodlands of the Mississippi and Ohio River Valleys shortly after the birth of Christ. But recent research has established the eastern woodlands of North America as another independent center of plant domestication, where about 4,000 years ago, long before maize was brought into the area, hunter-gatherer societies planted and harvested grasses such as goosefoot, marsh elder, and sunflowers. For a long time in this area, however, agriculture was of secondary importance, and people still depended upon wild deer, turkeys, small mammals, fish, and birds for their food. Farming in the eastern United States did not become essential to Native American communities until about 1,000 years ago. But certainly by the time of European contact, Indian communities throughout eastern North America farmed and fed themselves on a balanced diet of corn, beans, and squash, mixed with fish and meat in the dish we call succotash. They also knew how to smoke their meat to preserve it, and they shredded it and mixed it with berries and animal fat into molds of pemmican—a rich source of fat, protein, and vitamins eaten when game was scarce.

Farmers and Tyrants

We can see how similar patterns developed in many of the centers of early civilization. In the Near East and in China and India, agricultural communities grew larger and larger around the fertile river valleys—the Tigris, the Euphrates, the Nile, the Indus, the Huang Ho, and the Yangtze—where large-scale organization and administration were required to manage the floodwaters and to maintain an elaborate system of dikes and irrigation canals. Out of these river valley or "hydraulic" economies, as historians have called them, there arose the first city-states and their autocratic rulers, supported by their armies and by priests and wise men who studied the heavens, devised calendars, and knew when the rivers would flood and when to plant and harvest. The tyrants in their city-states ruled over the surrounding farmlands and encouraged a sense of national identity among their subjects. They also dreamed of conquering the farmlands of their neighbors. The first grass-fed civilizations experienced a long period of warfare and consolidation, as almost every city-state, sooner or later, suffered siege and destruction in the building up of greater and greater empires.

Each of these empires was sustained by a highly organized workforce tilling the land and a set of religious and cultural values that reinforced the discipline of agricultural activity, including the practice of fertility rituals, worship of the king as a sun-god, or belief in a philosophy such as Confucianism, which preached obedience to superiors. Though individual empires arose and disappeared, the basic pattern of political organization, shaped by the demands of agriculture, was passed on to succeeding societies. Most people worked as farmers, their surplus grain taken to feed the king, his administrators and soldiers, his accountants and tax collectors, and all the laborers and craftsmen required to build his cities. The need for protection from foreign invasion, as well as the prosperity and population increase engendered by successful agricultural organization, convinced the farmers that the state had to be at least tolerated. They saw that their survival was bound to the wisdom or god-like powers of their tyrant rulers, and they believed that a portion of their wealth should rightly be given to their superiors for the public good. So they accepted their place as lowly tillers. The farmers had carried out a dramatic revolution in human society, growing enough food for the kings and their cities, and as a result they promptly lost control of history. The story of agriculture is in part the story of how the farmers who feed us all came to be among the lowest and poorest members of the social order.

In addition to civilization and warfare, agriculture brought one new experience to people—famine. Starvation had plagued the hunter-gatherers, but this was something new, on a scale never seen before. It was a threat to the whole civilization and its future, and it could break the social compact and topple rulers. The new empires, with their city-states of 50,000 to

200,000 people, were completely dependent upon the surplus harvest. Every few years, the floods would fail to come, or insects would ravage the crops, or marauding armies would destroy the fields. And when the harvest failed, the effects were devastating. Many starved and others died of the diseases that thrived among the undernourished and the unburied dead. The countryside grew quiet, and the city-state became first a place of violence and riot, and then a place of grim silence. The gods had deserted the king and the nation, and the people were cursed. Civilization evaporated.

The earliest known reference to famine comes from Egypt around 3,500 B.C. A more recent Egyptian famine in A.D. 1064 resulted in widespread cannibalism. In 436 B.C. in Rome, starving people threw themselves into the Tiber river. In China in A.D. 1333, millions died, and the plague that followed spread to Europe where it was known as the Black Death. The worst famine on record occurred in China between 1876 and 1879, when as many as 13 million people may have died. In ancient societies, the importance of storing grain for a bad year was learned from bitter experience. The biblical story of Joseph, who was sold into slavery in Egypt by his brothers, but who rose to become one of the Pharaoh's most trusted ministers by predicting seven years of abundance followed by seven years of famine, was based upon common knowledge of the rhythms of the Nile and must have been deeply affecting for those who had lived through lean years.

Grossly oversimplifying, we may summarize by saying that between 8,000 and 4,000 B.C., in three different regions of the world—the Near East, the Far East, and Middle America—with three varieties of grass—wheat, rice, and corn—the hunter-gatherers turned themselves into settled farmers, producing such surpluses of grain that, by the end of this period, great civilizations had arisen in each region. These centers of agricultural abundance also became targets for conflict and predation. Between 7,000 and 4,000 years ago, the population of the world had increased from 3 million to more than 100 million. The agricultural revolution had produced so many more mouths to feed that the food resources of others were coveted.

In the Near East and Asia, the farmers were under constant pressure from the "barbarians," the nomadic pastoralists of the northern temperate zone, the Scythians and Thracians of the Mediterranean, the Gauls and Germanic peoples of northern Europe, and the fierce mounted cavalry of the Mongols. The Mongols would begin their conquest of China in the late thirteenth century. The Thracians became the Greeks, who by 330 B.C. under Alexander the Great would conquer the entire Fertile Crescent. The Roman Empire would conquer parts of it again before the birth of Christ, and the Muslim Empire would absorb it in the seventh century.

Not all societies were self-sufficient in producing food. The Greeks had developed a maritime civilization based on trading. Their land was too poor to grow all the wheat and barley they needed as their population began to grow, so they exchanged the few products they were able to grow for the food of their neighbors. They had transformed a scrawny wild bush first found in the mountains of the Fertile Crescent into the olive tree, whose roots could survive in the dry, rocky soil of the northern Mediterranean coast. The olives were not only eaten, but their oil was used in lamps for light. Another plant that grew well in the rocky soil was the grape vine, and the Greeks became masters of winemaking. They shipped their wine all over the Mediterranean in *amphorae*, huge clay jars with pointed bottoms so that they could be stuck in the sand to keep them upright. One of their biggest customers were the Gauls to the northwest, and the Greeks established the city of Massilia, on the present-day site of Marseilles, to encourage this trade. In this way, winemaking spread into France.

Feeding Rome

The last great civilization of antiquity, Rome, chose conquest over trade to solve its food problems. The Etruscans had fought the Greeks for the wheatfields of southern Italy, and won, but the indigenous Italian people had driven out the Etruscan kings around 500 B.C. and established their own

A Roman feast was usually an extravagant affair, afforded only by the wealthy.

nation. But Italy is primarily a mountainous country, with the same poor soil as other Mediterranean regions, and the small amount of arable land in the south could not feed its growing population. So the Romans created a formidable army that marched out in all directions in search of wheat. The legions marched north as far as England, France, and Germany, but the yields of wheat and barley were low in northern Europe and the soldiers needed more than they could obtain locally. Feeding the armies became a logistical nightmare, and the Romans had to build many forts and stock them with as much as a year's supply of grain in order to maintain their control of these areas.

The legions also marched south and east, and here they gained control of the Fertile Crescent and, in Julius Caesar's time, Egypt. From this point on, grain ships from Egypt and the other eastern provinces fed the Romans, but conquest by force was a double-edged sword. If a province rebelled, if barbarians threatened the supply lines, or if the grain shipments were late, there was panic in Rome. A fleet of galleys was kept near Naples for the sole purpose of patrolling the eastern Mediterranean and guarding the grain ships. More legions were required to ensure the flow of food to Rome, and the legions themselves demanded more food in a vicious circle. The cost of protecting the conquered provinces of the Roman Empire and the taxes imposed to pay for this protection became an ever increasing burden for the Romans.

The average Roman subsisted mostly on wheat and olives, but the upper classes, the patricians, were real epicures. A Roman named Apicius wrote the first cookbook and supposedly killed himself when he felt that his dwindling fortune would no longer provide him with the sumptuous meals he was accustomed to. The Roman general Lucullus once spent the equivalent of $90,000 on one meal for two guests. Of course, the guests were statesmen Pompey and Cicero. The Romans appropriated the finest and most exotic foods from their far-ranging provinces, and they perfected the art of the feast and the dinner party. They even invented a word for the professional dinner guest who frequently managed to get himself invited to other people's tables—the "parasite." The wealthy Roman brought his guests into a special dining room in his home or villa where the guests reclined on couches while they ate. First courses included olives, sausages flavored with pepper, plums, pomegranates, and oysters. A course of game followed—capons, ducks, rabbits, and partridge—and a course of fish followed the game. The meat dish came next, and the meal ended with pastries, sweetmeats, dates, and almonds. Everything was washed down with wine. Onions, peppers, and exotic spices from every corner of the known world flavored the dishes. The spices were expensive, because the Romans had to sail all the way to India to get them, but then as now, the affluent relished imported foods.

After a time, the costs of maintaining the empire became unmanageable. The armies required more and more food, as did the Roman citizens. Growing class divisions at home had impoverished many farmers, and the emperors kept the peace by doling out free food. At the gladiatorial combats in the arena, spectators were given a *sportula*, a lunch box full of pork, bread, oil, and wine, and the satirist Juvenal wrote that "Rome is governed by bread and circuses." At the time of Julius Caesar's death, more than 300,000 Romans were receiving free food from the state, and this, along with the cost of the legions, began to drain the imperial treasury. In the final years of their decline, the emperors took drastic measures. They regulated the price of bread and forced the bakers into a hereditary caste to control their activities. Finally, they ended the free distribution of food to the plebeians, as the common people were called. The social compact broke down, the legions' supply lines became tenuous, and the nomadic pastoralists of northern Europe were able to sweep down into Italy and destroy the empire.

Chapter Three
Food and Civilization

The Romans had been cruel oppressors, but they had built up and maintained a system of international trade around the Mediterranean region and beyond that had become indispensable to the civilization of Europe and its food resources. With the collapse of the Roman Empire, political organization, trade, and economic activity declined throughout Western Europe. The "barbarians" who conquered Rome, the nomadic pastoralists with their mounted cavalry, adopted Christianity and settled down to become the princes and nobles of medieval Europe. They ruled over communities of farmers, now called peasants, who were organized into largely self-sufficient manorial estates. From their imposing manor houses and castles, the lords provided protection from bandits and invading armies. The peasants lived in nearby villages and worked in the fields every day, cultivating their crops or grazing their animals. They shared the villages with the lord's craftsmen—blacksmiths and metal workers, tanners, millers, bakers, woodworkers, and stonemasons. The small-scale and self-sufficient structure of the basic agro-political unit—the feudal estate—and the many kingdoms, dukedoms, and baronies built upon it, resulted from the absence of a central organizing authority after the collapse of Rome. In the absence of safe and stable international trade, the people of northern Europe were dependent on their own land for food.

Life for the medieval farmer was difficult. The soils of northern Europe were poor, the climate was quite cold, and the growing season was short. Agricultural techniques were primitive, and yields were modest compared to the amount of human labor required for planting and harvesting. As late as the seventeenth century, Europeans experienced food shortages about every three years and genuine famine every decade. Each peasant family cultivated between 6 to 30 acres (2.4 to 12 ha). By comparison, an American farm family during the colonial period could cultivate as much as 200 acres (81 ha). The peasant was also required to farm the lord's land and perform various labor services for him. Aside from his own lands, the lord took about one-sixth of the harvest from the peasants' fields through a variety of taxes. Though a seemingly small portion, it was enough, considering the low level of agricultural productivity, to ensure that few peasants could accumulate much wealth or rise above their position. The peasants were not unaware of the exploitative relationship between tillers and lords, and they did not always accept their lot. During a peasant rebellion in England in 1381, a man named John Ball preached a sermon in which he blasted the lords, "They have wine and spices and fair bread, and we have oat cake and straw and water to drink. They have leisure and fine houses; we have pain and labor, the rain and wind in the fields. And yet it is of us and of our toil that these men hold their state."[1] Martin Luther's Protestant revolution of 1517 could not have succeeded without the support of the peasants, who associated their oppression with the Roman Catholic princes of the German states.

The shipments of wheat from the eastern and southern Mediterranean countries had ceased, and in some areas of northern Europe people came to depend on barley, rye, and oats for their basic food crops. These cereals made poor breads, and bread made from wheat became very expensive and was found mostly on the tables of the wealthy. The peasants could not even make their own bread in many cases, because the millers and the bakers worked for the lord and charged the farmers for their services. Olive oil also became rare, and people learned to burn animal fats as a source of light and to flavor their bread with butter instead. The lord also controlled the wine presses, and poorer folk drank beer and mead, a beverage fermented from honey. Honey was the only commonly available sweetener for foods. Fruits such as apples, cherries, peaches, and a variety of berries were available, but citrus fruits such as oranges and lemons were virtually unknown. On small private plots, the peasants could grow vegetables and keep some chickens and geese. Most food was served finely chopped or minced or hashed, or in the form of porridges, soups, and stews. Meat was cut by the cook or carver, not by the diner. People ate with their hands, because forks and spoons did not come into general use until the early sixteenth century. The first flat dinner plates did not appear until the late 1530s, so people ate off wooden boards or piled their food onto thick slices of bread.

Food and Feudalism

At first, meat was not as rare as is commonly thought, even on the tables of the poor, because there was abundant game in the forests and a flourishing cattle trade with the regions of eastern Europe. Cattle and oxen, however, were still scrawny and were used mostly to pull the primitive plows across the fields. The lords took possession of the forests and declared them off-limits to commoners, making poachers of all who hunted there. Kings and princes decreed "sumptuary laws" that forbid common people from eating certain animals such as deer, swans, peacocks, and cormorants. In England, even today, all swans are the property of the queen, and each year they are rounded up and marked in a ritual known as swan upping. The enclosure of the forests caused much friction between the nobles and the commoners, and outlaws such as the legendary Robin Hood lived in the forest and killed the king's deer in defiance of the sumptuary laws.

The real decline in meat consumption on the part of the poor, however, came somewhat later, in the middle of the sixteenth century. By this time, the population of Europe had recovered from the Black Death, the bubonic plague that had swept through Europe in the middle of the fourteenth century. Rising populations put increasing pressure on an unproductive agricultural system, causing grain prices to skyrocket, which raised the cost of feeding livestock. Divisions of wealth were also increasing as the nobles were consolidating their power just prior to the age of the great monarchies. It was at this time that meat began to disappear from the peasant's diet. A person's social status could now be determined not only by what he did, but by what he ate.

In the Christian monasteries that sprang up all over Europe, the monks and nuns ate the diet of the poor. The Christians believed that one of the reasons the Roman Empire had collapsed was because of its gluttony and excess, and they determined to live and eat simply. They also believed in hard work, and their industriousness in agriculture preserved many foods from Roman times, especially wine. Wine was thought to have medicinal properties during the Middle Ages, and drinking it was not considered sinful. Indeed, the Europeans had little choice because of the poor quality of their water. The monasteries and their vineyards were famous throughout Europe, as was their hospitality to travelers at a time when inns and stopping places were few and far between. The making of wine is a fairly simple process in which yeast cells, which come to rest on the skins of the grapes, eat the sugar in the juice of the crushed grapes and turn it into alcohol. The higher the sugar content of the grapes, the higher the final level of alcohol. When the alcohol content reaches about 13 percent to 15 percent, it kills the yeast cells, the fermentation stops, and the wine is considered stable. The monks diligently pruned the vines, cutting off many of the new shoots so that the vines produced fewer grapes with a higher sugar con-

Christian monks believed in hard work, and many of them pursued their efforts in agriculture.

tent. Today, when a harvest of grapes has a low sugar content, pure sugar is added to the fermenting grape juice in a process known as chaptilization. This is considered "cheating" by wine connoisseurs and is forbidden by law in some countries, though there is no difference in the taste of the wine. Their vineyards saved many of the monasteries from destruction when parts of the continent—Spain, eastern Europe—were overrun by the Muslims. They were the one place where a local Muslim ruler, forbidden by his religion to consume alcoholic beverages, could sneak off for a drink.

The diet of the nobility, as one would expect, was much more elaborate than that of the peasants or the Christian brotherhoods. Food played a very special role in the political life of the feudal lords. Early medieval society was for the most part a cashless society, where barter and obligatory service took the place of money. For the nobleman, food was an essential element in cementing the loyalties of his vassals. The ruler of every manor house or castle was expected to keep an open kitchen, where guests, visitors, or almost anyone from the feudal estate who was in need could stop by for a portion of meat, bread, and beer, served in a quantity and style according to his or her station. Some of the great lords fed thousands every day and could in turn expect service and devotion from these diners. Important guests sat at "high table" at the head of the lord's great hall, and those of lesser rank sat at "low table." This distinction has been preserved in the dining halls of the older English universities.

The tradition of feasting and banqueting had not been forgotten, and when the occasion was important enough or the guest of high enough rank, the banquet could be extravagant. The menu might include prodigious amounts of bread made from wheat, along with wine, ale, beef, lamb, pork, venison, game birds, fish, seal and whale meat, jellies, candies, and custards. The custards were not like today's desserts, but contained meat and fish and were served as main courses. Candies, incidentally, got their name from Candia in Crete, one of the few places from which feudal Europe could import sugar. For feasts, animals might be killed and freshly roasted, but for everyday meals, meat was taken from the storeroom where it had been placed in casks after smoking or salting or pickling it in brine to preserve it. Knights and their retainers lived on this smoked or salted meat, especially on military campaigns. Salt not only helped to preserve meat but also enhanced its flavor. It was also important in preparing the fish brought in by early European fishing fleets from the North and Norwegian Seas. These uses made salt very valuable.

The Search for Spice

Spices, too, were highly valued, because they made the poor-quality meats and vegetables more flavorful. They not only made food more flavorful, but Arab doctors, highly respected in medieval Europe, had convinced people that spices were powerful medicines, able to prevent infections, increase longevity, and promote virility. Those who could afford them lavished a variety of exotic spices on their food—pepper, saffron, fennel, parsley, sage, thyme, cinnamon, ginger, basil, mint, dill, nutmeg, coriander, cardamom, cloves, oregano, turmeric, mace, and cumin. Medieval recipes are famous for their rich combinations of such spices. But flavorful cooking was only for the wealthy nobility. The porridges and gruels that graced the table of the peasant family were quite tasteless.

The feudal lords' demand for spices and other luxuries would eventually undermine their rule and revolutionize the economy of western Europe. Spices came from the Far East—China, Japan, India, and Southeast Asia. Unlike the Romans, and in spite of their crusades, the princes of Europe had no authority over the trade routes and had to pay others to bring the spices to them. First there was the long and costly overland journey across the Silk Route to get them from Asia to the port of Aleppo in modern-day Syria, where Arab merchants and Venetian traders took them across the Mediterranean and added to their price. In the fifteenth century, the Ottoman Turks, fiercely hostile to Christianity, took over the trade routes across the Near East and raised the price of spices by more than 800 percent. The lords were desperate for their spices, and more than 2,500 tons (2,268 mt) of spices were shipped from Aleppo to Venice every year, with the meager currency reserves of the European nobility going the other way.

Free Labor

The need for cash encouraged the lords to improve the productivity of their estates, but the peasantry had no incentive to work harder if all the benefits went to the lord's table. To get more out of the land, the lords began to hire free-wage laborers, and some of the peasants were allowed to work off the land as craftsmen, making goods such as woven textiles that could be traded for spices. During the fourteenth century, when the Black Death swept across Europe and killed one-third of its population, the price of free labor rose as the nobility had to compete for the services of the surviving workers. All this created opportunities for ambitious commoners and industrious craftsmen to prosper, and some of the villages grew into towns, and the towns into cities, and the free men and women in the towns and cities became wealthy and powerful enough to challenge the unlimited political authority of the nobility.

The cities represented a new way of life—and places from which trade and a greater political consciousness could be revived. Though the lords taxed their free markets, they could never fully control them. A far-sighted lord might form an alliance with the cities, endorsing policies designed to promote their economic growth while exploiting their wealth and power to extend his rule. Such a lord might rise above other lords to command a kingdom. But most of the nobles fought a long, losing battle against the towns and cities, the value of their land rapidly decreasing when set against the value of the manufactures in the money economy of the burghers (middle class). Once he lost control of the towns, all the lord had was the land, and his income was shackled to an unproductive agricultural system. The townspeople, on the other hand, had learned a valuable lesson. If you could make and sell things, you didn't need to work the land; you could purchase the food you needed. You could, in fact, buy whatever you wanted, including a militia to protect the town from the lord's soldiers. Free-wage labor and the resulting incentive to higher productivity, the comfort and security of urban life, and the rise of free markets and the cash economy all produced changes in people's thinking about the rights and privileges assumed by the nobles over them. The desire to flavor their food with expensive imported spices had compelled the nobility to tolerate the existence of economic forces that they couldn't control, disturbing the stability of their self-sufficient manorial system and creating the basis for modern capitalism.

One problem that the early cities struggled with was providing clean and safe drinking water. Water came from rivers, lakes, wells, or cisterns that collected the rain. Some of the better-planned cities used aqueducts, water wheels, and simple pumps in conjunction with systems of terra-cotta or lead pipes to bring water in. But many cities lacked these systems, and thousands of the poor found employment as water-haulers all over Europe. There were 20,000 water-haulers working in Paris up until the eighteenth century, bringing water from the city's principal source, the Seine, throughout the city and to the upper floors of the new, higher buildings. And water from the Seine was of dubious quality. Dye-makers, tanners, and other craftsmen dumped their waste into the river. Some people added a few drops of vinegar to their water to kill the unpleasant taste. With no understanding of how disease is spread and fairly primitive sewage systems, city people could mysteriously die from a drink of water. It was no wonder that wine and beer were the preferred drinks.

Europe Reaches Out

In their desperation for flavorful food, the princes of Europe searched for a way to circumvent the Mediterranean trading monopolies of the Venetians and the Turks and to get at the spices directly. They read about the riches of the Far East in the journal of the merchant-explorer Marco Polo, who had returned from the court of Kublai Khan in 1295. "I assure you," he had written, "that for one shipload of pepper that goes to Alexandria or elsewhere to be taken to Christian lands, there comes an hundred to the port of Canton."[2] If a sea route to the Far East could be dis-

Hundreds of years ago, the water in Paris was not of good quality since craftsmen dumped their waste into the rivers.

covered, Europe could regain control of the spice trade. The search for spices launched the great age of European exploration, the revival of interest in science and learning, and the rise of predatory mercantile states with powerful navies and new dreams of empire.

Christopher Columbus was one of the men who read Marco Polo's book. Working for the Spanish king Ferdinand, he sought a new route to the riches of Asia by sailing west from Europe across the Atlantic. Instead, he discovered the Americas, in four voyages between 1492 and 1503, but all his life he refused to believe that he had not landed on the coast of Cypangu, or Japan. No matter, because the riches of the Americas more than compensated the Spanish empire for his failure. There were enormous quantities of gold and silver to be mined in Central America, and the Caribbean had rich farmland that the indigenous people could be enslaved to work. The discovery of the New World also exposed both continents to new foods. The Spaniards brought grapes, lemons, oranges, sugar cane, pigs, horses, and cattle from Europe. They brought back to Europe the foods they found the Indians growing—cassava, various beans and peppers, pineapples, peanuts, cacao, potatoes, tomatoes, and, of course, corn.

Both the potato and the tomato fared poorly when they arrived in Europe, and for a long time they were not fully accepted as food plants. Both were recognized as members of the *Solanaceae*, or nightshade, family, related to poisonous plants such as henbane, mandrake, and belladonna, so Europeans may have been reluctant to eat them for this reason. Indeed, if exposed to light while growing, potatoes turn green and poisonous. Farmers are conservative about trying out new food plants in any case. The story is that Louis XVI of France convinced the peasants of the value of the potato by posting an armed guard around a field planted with them outside Paris. The curiosity of the peasants was aroused by the king's effort to protect this mysterious plant. Louis withdrew his guards at night, and soon all the potatoes had been dug up and stolen. Soon the potato, the *pomme de terre*, the "apple of the earth," was growing throughout France, and eventually the rest of Europe. Sir Walter Raleigh introduced the potato into England and Ireland in 1588.

Corn was also accepted only slowly, because the Europeans did not know how to eat it. The Indians mixed it with beans, squash, fish, and meat, but the Europeans tried to eat it in great quantities without other dishes and suffered from pellagra because of corn's low protein content. The Europeans called corn "Indian corn," or used the Indian name of maize, because corn was the name they had given to their own cereal grains. In European accounts written before the modern era, when the reader encounters the word corn, the writer is actually referring to wheat, barley, or rye. Efforts to promote the growing of potatoes and corn in Europe were not made out of benevolence toward the peasantry, but to provide them with a cheap source of food, which the nobility hoped would stave off revolution.

The Portuguese were in competition with the Spanish for the spice trade, and under the leadership of Prince Henry, known as the "Navigator," Portuguese explorers began to sail south down the west coast of Africa, looking for a way to get around the continent and head east for India. They were encouraged by the discovery of pepper growing along the east African coast, and the discovery of gold in Mauritania. In 1498, Vasco da Gama sailed around the Cape of Good Hope at the southern tip of Africa and anchored off the east coast of India. It was the first time in 1,000 years, since the days of the Roman Empire, that a European ship had reached India, and the Arab and Turkish traders were alarmed. The eastern potentates of the Muslim empire formed a fleet to stop the Portuguese but were defeated at the Battle of Diu in 1509, and the Portuguese gained control of the spice trade, having circumvented the overland routes to Europe. They monopolized trade with China, India, Japan, and the Spice Islands—Java, Sumatra, and the Moluccas. They controlled the trade in pepper, ginger, cloves, cinnamon, and nutmeg. The Spanish struck back when the ships of Ferdinand Magellan, a Portuguese explorer working for the King Charles I of Spain, sailed west around the southern tip of South America, across the

Sir Walter Raleigh was responsible for bringing the potato to England and Ireland.

Pacific Ocean, and landed in the Mariana Islands in 1521, picking up a cargo of spices and leaving quickly before the Portuguese could discover their presence.

Spice Wars

Other nations entered the competition. The Spanish had worked to death many of the indigenous people of the Caribbean islands on their sugar-cane plantations, and were now importing slaves from Africa to do the planting and harvesting. The English had been participating in this slave trade alongside the Spanish, until the Spanish viceroy of Mexico attacked the ships of the English slave trader John Hawkins. The English went to war against Spain, attacking Spanish fortresses in the Americas, and one of the sailors who had been with Hawkins, Francis Drake, in addition to his other exploits, sailed to the Moluccas. There he exploited local resentments against the religiously intolerant Portuguese and Spanish and opened the spice trade to England. By 1588, with the destruction of a Spanish invasion force off the coast of Plymouth, the English had effectively crushed the Spanish empire, which was close to bankruptcy anyway due to its constant wars against competitors. Drake, incidentally, was also the first to try to find the Northwest Passage, the dreamed-of sea route across North America to Asia, again motivated by a desire to control the spice trade.

The Dutch, too, had been fighting to free themselves from Spanish domination in northern Europe, with English help. After 1580, when the Spanish had taken control of Portugal, the Dutch began to attack Portuguese fortresses in Brazil, Africa, and the Spice Islands. They defeated the Portuguese in a naval battle off Java in 1602 and formed the Dutch East India Company to manage the spice trade. The Dutch republic had embraced wholeheartedly the values of democratic capitalism, and their trading company was managed by the stockholders. Every Dutch burgher could make a contribution and expect a share of the profits, and the Dutch

East India Company was wealthier than any king in Europe, able to build its own fleets, equip its armies, and maintain fortresses throughout the Far East. The markets for Asian spices shifted from Venice and Lisbon to Amsterdam. The Dutch stranglehold on the spice trade raised the price of pepper in London markets, and the English retaliated by forming their own British East India Company, defeating the Portuguese in naval battles off the coast of northeast Australia and taking possession of some of the Spice Islands. But in 1623 the Dutch drove them out of the region, and the English retreated west to concentrate on their investments in India. The Dutch maintained their monopoly over the spice trade until the late eighteenth century, when American ships entered Asian waters. Operating out of the shallow harbor of Salem, Massachusetts, the American ships were smaller and drew less water than European vessels, and they could sail upriver to Asian ports the Europeans could not reach. With the coming of the Americans, the spice trade was finally opened up to all nations, and prices were no longer controlled by the old mercantile monopolies.

Nutrition at Sea

The dependence of nation-states on navies and fleets of trading ships during this period created new food problems for the Europeans—how to properly feed the crews on long sailing voyages. Starvation was common on board ship, and sometimes the majority of the sailors and passengers did not survive the voyage. A sailor's ration usually consisted of salted meat, which goes bad quickly in warm climates, and rock-hard biscuits, which were often infected with insects. Water casks were often filled from the sewage-laden rivers of the home ports, and the water turned foul in the moldy holds of the vessels, so sailors preferred to drink beer or rum. The traditional sailor's grog of the British Royal Navy was one part rum and two parts water, issued every day. Drunkenness caused many a tragedy at sea. The human body, furthermore, can store vitamin C for only three or four months, and if no fresh fruit or meat is consumed on longer voyages, the symptoms of scurvy, the "sailor's disease," appear—loosening of the teeth, bleeding, dementia, and ultimately death. For a long time, this disease ravaged the navies of Europe. In 1753, the British naval surgeon James Lind conducted a number of experiments and in his *A Treatise on the Scurvy* he declared that fresh fruit or fruit juice would make the disease disappear. Lind's advice, however, was ignored by the notoriously rigid Royal Navy until the voyages of Captain James Cook. Cook forced his men to eat sauerkraut and to drink lemon juice, and on three long sea voyages around the world he did not lose a single sailor to scurvy. Thereafter British sailors drank a ration of lime juice to ward off scurvy and became known as "limeys." The exact nature of these diseases as vitamin deficiencies was not understood until the twentieth century, however. As late as 1912, Captain Robert Falcon Scott, making a four-month journey across the frozen wastes of Antarctica to the South Pole and back, neglected to provide his expedition with a source of vitamin C, and all five members of the polar party died, in part from the effects of scurvy.

The Power of Trade

Over several centuries, the search for spices and other exotic goods had transformed feudal Europe from a fragmented and undernourished agrarian society into a group of powerful states dependent on manufacturing and maritime trade for survival. Most of these states were strong monarchies; a few, like Holland and England, were republics governed by propertied men. All were aggressive and entrepreneurial in spirit and willing to go to war to get what they wanted. Free trade was not practiced. Under the prevailing economic philosophy of mercantilism, each state imported only the raw materials it needed, while exporting manufactured goods at higher value. Other country's products were blocked from entry if they competed with locally made products. The first inequities in modern global trading patterns began to appear as the agricultural societies of Africa, Asia, and the New World became colonial reserves for the foods the Europeans craved.

Chocolate, Coffee, and Tea

Many of the foods that figured so prominently in this transition were not basic sources of nourishment at all, but stimulants and other foods that are not strictly necessary to the human diet. We have already mentioned spices. Others were chocolate, coffee, tea, and sugar. Chocolate comes from the pod of the cacao tree, first discovered by the Spaniards when Hernán Cortéz conquered the Aztec Empire of Mexico. It is rich in starch, protein, and oil. The cacao pods were extremely valuable, and the Mayas used them for currency. The Indians ground the pods and prepared the chocolate in the form of a thick, cold syrup, sometimes adding corn to it. But the Europeans, because of its expense, watered it down and served it as a hot drink. Chocolate contains the stimulant theobromine, and at first the Europeans regarded it as an aphrodisiac that made women reckless with their virtue, but by the eighteenth century these prejudices faded and the drink became very popular.

Tea and coffee contain the stimulant caffeine, an insecticide developed by the plants to keep themselves from being eaten, which accounts for the bitter taste of drinks that contain it. Tea and coffee were appreciated because they promoted wakefulness and alertness. Tea comes from the leaves of the *Camelia sinensis* plant, a bush native to China and India that was supposedly discovered by the Chinese emperor Shen Nung in 2,737 B.C. After the leaves of the tea bush are picked, they may be quickly dried by fire in a shallow bowl, which produces green tea, still popular in China, or they can be dried by the heat of the sun, which causes the leaves to ferment and darken, producing the black tea more popular in the West.

Tea was first brought to Europe by the Dutch in 1610. The tea was

Coffeehouses became popular meeting places in European cities.

expensive, but it was one of the first nonalcoholic beverages that people could drink regularly, and because it was prepared with boiling water it was safe to drink. In the 1830s, the Americans built a new kind of sailing ship, the clipper ship, slim and streamlined with a great spread of sail. The clipper ships were very fast and became essential to the tea trade. They took immigrants from the east coast of the Americas around Cape Horn to the

California goldfields, and then sailed to the port of Canton in China to pick up a cargo of tea, which was then taken to London. Their speed reduced the cost of the voyage and made tea more affordable to the Europeans.

Coffee probably originated in Ethiopia and arrived in Europe about the middle of the seventeenth century. Coffee became the stimulant of the scholar and the businessman and the office clerk keeping late hours. It was served in coffeehouses, of which there were more than 3,000 in London by 1700. Paris, Vienna, Berlin, and other European cities were also famous for their coffeehouses. Here businessmen and intellectuals gathered to sip coffee, discuss the day's events, and read the newspapers that coffeehouses provided for free. One of the most famous coffeehouses in Paris was the Procope, which became popular when the Comédie-Française opened across the street in 1686. Its patrons in later years included Diderot and Voltaire. The members of certain professions made some coffeehouses their favorite haunts, and here information could be exchanged and deals could be made in an atmosphere of lively bourgeois camaraderie. A curious evolution took place in which some of these coffeehouses became formal centers of business and trade, where pledges to buy and sell became binding and where market prices were actually determined. The great banking and insurance firm, Lloyds of London, began as Lloyd's Coffeehouse.

Sugar

Before beet sugar was discovered, all sugar was derived from the sugar-cane plant, which originally came from India and was introduced into the Mediterranean region by the Persians. Sugar is pure carbohydrate, a source of energy but nothing else. Other foods can provide human beings with the necessary carbohydrates, along with proteins and vitamins as well, but the Europeans became addicted to the sweetening effect of sugar in their foods and in their new chocolate, coffee, and tea beverages. They also discovered how to ferment and distill sugar into rum.

The Spaniards brought sugar cane to the West Indies with their conquest of the New World. But the process of making sugar was a laborious one in which the cane stalks had to be cut and crushed and the juice squeezed out of them and then boiled down into syrup and finally cooled into crystals of pure sugar. The Spanish conquistadors did not come to the New World to do this kind of labor themselves, and they enslaved the native Caribs and Arawaks of the islands to work on their plantations. Harvesting cane was brutal work, and most of the Indians died or rebelled against their brutal overseers. Looking for a new source of cheap labor, the Spaniards turned to the Portuguese colonies of Africa and began to trade their manufactures to local African chiefs in exchange for slaves. It was not long before English and French planters in the Caribbean, as well as colonial planters in Virginia, anxious to grow tobacco for export to England, faced a similar labor shortage when their indentured servants finished their terms of servitude and moved on. The English and French followed the example of the Spaniards and imported Africans to work their fields. Thus the institution of slavery spread throughout the Caribbean and the southern United States. Wealthy British and New England merchants became involved, providing the ships that carried slaves, sugar, and rum back and forth across the Atlantic in what came to be known as the Triangle of Trade. Ships would leave Liverpool and Newport loaded with trade goods to exchange in Africa for slaves. The slaves were taken across the Atlantic in a voyage called the Middle Passage. The slaves were unloaded in the Caribbean islands, and the ships were then stocked up with sugar and molasses for the voyage back to Europe or America.

There is an interesting historical footnote to the story of Caribbean sugar and slavery. In 1789, the crew of the English ship H.M.S. *Bounty* mutinied against their captain, William Bligh, after leaving the island of Tahiti, and put him in a small boat and cast him adrift. Bligh was a harsh master, but so were most English sea captains of the time, and it was probably the seductions of Tahiti rather than the harsh discipline that drove the sailors to rebel. In any case, Bligh had sailed to Tahiti before with Captain Cook, and there he had encountered the breadfruit tree, whose fruit was rich in carbohydrate. The mission of the *Bounty* had been to transplant the breadfruit to the Caribbean islands as a cheap source of food for the slaves on the sugar plantations. Bligh survived the mutiny and on another voyage in 1792 he finally managed to bring the trees to the West Indies, but the slaves rejected the new food in favor of indigenous foods like the banana, sensing that the breadfruit was part of a plan to work them even harder.

With the decline of the Spanish empire, England and France fought desperately for control of the Caribbean, and it was their hope of regaining control of the sugar plantations of the West Indies that pushed the French to support the American revolution against England. After the fleet of the Comte de Grasse had helped to cut off Cornwallis's retreat at Yorktown, forcing his surrender to George Washington, the French fleet sailed south into the Caribbean to drive out the English. But the French admiral was defeated and the West Indies remained firmly in British hands. This posed serious problems for France's sugar industry, and in the early 1800s Napoleon encouraged research into the extraction of sugar from beets, and a substitute for sugar cane was found.

The world paid for the sweetness of sugar with one of the bitterest forms of human exploitation ever devised. Twenty million Africans were uprooted and carried off into slavery in the three and a half centuries of the slave trade. The effort to abolish slavery often took the form of an attack on the sugar industry.

Sugar was boycotted, and abolitionists sweetened their coffee with cream instead. One abolitionist organization was known as the Anti-Saccharite Society. Finally, in 1806, the British foreign secretary Charles Fox forbade the use of British ships for the slave trade, and finally in 1833 slavery was abolished throughout the British Empire.

American Empire

By the 1840s, the sugar industry in the West Indies was losing its importance. Boston merchants had rediscovered Captain Cook's Sandwich Islands, the islands of Hawaii, as another group of subtropical islands capable of supporting sugar cane. Huge cane plantations were established here, and the owners brought in as a workforce thousands of immigrants from China, Japan, Korea, India, and the Philippines. Sugar has given Hawaii its unique multi-ethnic composition, just as sugar transformed the ethnic mix of the West Indies from indigenous Indian to predominantly African. The motivation of the cane growers was not to produce racial harmony, however, but to set each ethnic group against the others in competition, so that wages could be kept low. Harvesting sugar cane was such difficult and unrewarding work that the children of each ethnic group, wanting a better life, abandoned the cane fields in favor of work in the cities or immigration to the United States. The growers then had to import a new nationality to maintain the workforce. In 1893, American planters helped to overthrow the government of Queen Liliuokalani, and in 1898 the United States formally took possession of the Hawaiian Islands. By 1903, a new crop was planted in the hills above the cane plantations, and men like James Dole grew rich exporting canned pineapples from the islands.

By the 1860s, as slavery and sugar cane in the West Indies were in decline, another food plant spread throughout the Caribbean. The banana, originally from India, had been introduced by the Spanish in the early 1500s. For a long time it remained only a local food, or on occasion it could be found on the tables of very wealthy Europeans. The problem was that the banana ripened fairly quickly after it was picked, and only with the greatest expense could it be shipped rapidly enough to market in foreign countries. The banana had to arrive still green, ripening just as it was offered for sale. The American clipper ships and Yankee entrepreneurship solved the problem. In 1870, the New England ship captain Lorenzo Dow Baker picked up a cargo of bananas and coconuts from Jamaica and, making good time on the trip home, sold them for a considerable profit in New Jersey. He encouraged Caribbean planters to grow more bananas, and eventually took control of the plantations and warehouses in Jamaica, Cuba, and Panama, forming the United Fruit Company in 1899. Bananas became a major export crop in these countries, as well as in Honduras, Costa Rica, Guatemala, and Nicaragua. The United Fruit Company built railroads, refineries, warehouses, port facilities, and power plants all over Central America to facilitate the rapid transport of fresh bananas to the world. So important was the banana trade to these economies, and so dominant were foreign companies such as United Fruit (now Chiquita Brands International) in controlling that trade and in manipulating the policies of local governments in their favor, that many Caribbean and Central American nations were cynically called "banana republics," and bananas themselves were called "green gold." Whether the crop was sugar cane or bananas or some other tropical fruit or vegetable, it was the fate of the West Indies, as well as many other regions of Central and South America, to produce cheap agricultural exports for the countries of the Northern Hemisphere, and to be economically and politically dominated by them until modern times.

Opium

Spices, chocolate, tea, coffee, and sugar all demonstrate that the world can be drastically reshaped by human appetites that have little to do with nutritious eating. The craving for narcotics has also shaped our history. Hallucinogenic extracts from plants were in use when humans were still hunter-gatherers, but the commercial production of addictive substances did not become of major importance until the nineteenth century, and it is intertwined with the history of food in unusual ways. The British demand for Chinese tea, for example, was enormous, but British merchants had little that they could sell back to China, a nation of peasants living in poverty, with no cash and little use for Western manufactures, governed by a small Mandarin aristocracy suspicious of Western influence. Yet to pay for the tea in cash would have produced the same balance-of-payments problem experienced by the Romans and the feudal nobility centuries earlier, allowing the wealth of England to flow to the East. The British knew that they could grow poppies and process the seeds into opium in their new colonies in India and Burma, however, and that if they could ship the opium into China and addict enough Chinese, they could pay for their tea.

British traders began to bring opium into the port of Canton, and though opium was illegal in China, through bribery and chicanery the British convinced the imperial officials to look the other way. Finally, in the 1840s, the emperor Dao Guang decided to enforce the laws, and the British went to war to enforce their right to sell opium. They won the war and pushed upon the Chinese government a humiliating treaty permitting the British open use of the country's major ports. The island city of Hong Kong, south of Canton, or Guangzhou as it is called today, was founded by British traders looking for a safe place to warehouse their opium before shipping it upriver, and some of Britain's most prestigious international trading houses and financial institutions began as opium traders in the Far East.

The Industrial Revolution

By the second half of the nineteenth century, the Industrial Revolution and the growth of world trade had transformed Europe and the United States from agrarian into urban economies. Cities became vastly powerful centers of industry, commerce, and accumulated wealth, as well as being the places from which nations were ruled. In Europe, the handicraft industries of the feudal lord's villages had become large urban factories powered by coal and steam. In the factories, continual innovation was the key to keeping costs down, producing more and better goods, and beating the competition. As the material conditions of life grew richer and there was more to be had, everyone had an incentive to work harder, and the millions of new workers living in the cities had to be fed. That would be accomplished by changes in agricultural production brought on by the Industrial Revolution and the spirit of innovation that pervaded the age. World food output was about to double, and populations would increase accordingly.

The first step in this process, in Europe, was the act of enclosure. The aristocracy still controlled much of the land, and sensing its increasing value they passed laws that drove out all the farmers working small strips and the squatters working marginal lands. Enclosure could be a brutal process, but many of the dispossessed peasants were absorbed into the growing cities, providing more workers for the factories and a ready market for the greater quantities of food that would now be grown. Large tracts of land could now be enclosed with fences and hedges and worked plantation-style with improved farming implements and the efficient use of minimum amounts of labor. In 1701, the Oxford law student Jethro Tull, forced to take up farming because of bad health, invented a seed drill that buried each seed in the ground individually—a vast improvement over scattering the seeds on the surface of the soil by hand—and he instituted the practice of planting in rows. The Viscount Townshend, a relative of Prime Minister Robert Walpole, planted new root crops such as turnips, which provided food for cattle through the winter season. Previously, all but a few breeding animals were slaughtered each fall because there was no fodder for the cattle after the harvest had been distributed. Now fresh meat and dairy products were available all year round, vastly improving people's health and their capacity to work. The English agriculturist Robert Bakewell began to selectively breed cattle, sheep, and horses for larger size and superior qualities. In America, Thomas Jefferson turned his Monticello estate into a laboratory for agricultural experiments. A new kind of landed gentry evolved, progressive in spirit, innovative, and anxious to establish model farms from which others could borrow improved techniques. Serfdom was disappearing from Western Europe, since free labor was more efficient and could be

Thomas Jefferson conducted agricultural experiments at his Monticello plantation.

hired and fired as needed, unlike the serf and his family, who belonged to the land and had to be fed by the landowner even in hard times.

Much of this agricultural revolution took place in the United States. Though planters in the Southern states used slaves and later sharecroppers were used in other parts of the country, most American farmers had never been peasants or serfs, but free individuals who owned their own land and would profit from improvements in agricultural technique. American farms were also relatively small units operated by family labor. There was so much available land that hired labor was scarce and expensive, because anyone who was willing to farm would much prefer to obtain and work his own land rather than work for someone else. With a labor force limited to the size of his family, the American farmer had no choice but to apply improved techniques if he wanted to increase his production. Improved farm machinery was the key. Because the seed heads of wheat and other cereal grains disperse with the wind when the plants are mature, it was necessary to cut the grain as quickly as possible at harvest time. In 1831, the Virginia blacksmith Cyrus McCormick invented the first mechanical reaper, allowing grain to be harvested much more rapidly and reducing losses from spoilage. In 1837, John Deere invented the self-scouring steel plow, and thus the tough prairie sod of the American Midwest could be farmed efficiently. Eli Whitney's cotton gin automated the removal of seeds from the cotton boll and reduced the amount of labor required to harvest the crop. New plows, harvesters, threshers, seed drills, dairy creamers, milking machines, and water pumps revolutionized agricultural production. The novelist Anthony Trollope, traveling in the United States in 1861, wrote about the ". . . rivers of wheat and rivers of maize ever running. I saw the men bathed in corn as they distributed it in its flow. I saw bins by the score laden with wheat, in each of which bins there was space for a comfortable residence. I breathed the flour, and drank the flour, and felt myself to be enveloped in a world of breadstuff. And then I believed, understood, and brought it home to myself as a fact, that here in the corn lands of Michigan, and amidst the bluffs of

Wisconsin, and on the high table plains of Minnesota, and the prairies of Illinois, had God prepared the food for the increasing millions of the Eastern world, as for the coming millions of the Western."[3]

Transporting Food

The Industrial Revolution also solved the problem of getting food from the farmer to the consumer, however far apart they were, thanks mainly to the invention of the steamboat and the steam locomotive. Railroads meant that perishable foods such as milk and fish could be brought to urban markets much more quickly and in better condition. Fish were often packed in sea ice for transport, and this increased their iodine content, preventing the disease known as goiter, which was common among people who lived far from the sea and rarely ate fish. Faster, cheaper transport meant lower food prices. The farmer now sold his harvest to merchants and middlemen in the cities. The merchants had no use for unsold food, and when the markets were glutted or when demand declined for any reason, they lowered their prices. These were the times when the poorer classes could bargain for food. And fluctuating prices would determine what and how much the farmers grew, binding their prosperity to the behavior of the marketplace.

In the 1870s, two rival Chicago businessmen, Philip Armour and Gustavus Swift, both began to ship sides of beef to the eastern cities in refrigerated railway cars, ending the practice of salting or smoking meat to preserve it, and reducing the cost of shipping live cattle and slaughtering them at their destination. Before the refrigerated railway car, every city maintained its own stockyards and slaughterhouses for cattle, usually near breweries, where the steers could be fed from the leftover slops of the brewing process. This arrangement was not only unsanitary, but it blanketed some areas of the cities with horrible odors. The refrigerated railway car also opened up eastern markets in the United States to the citrus-growing regions of Florida and California. Florida was closer, but subject to frequent frosts that destroyed the fruit harvest. The climate was drier and milder in California, and by 1900 hundreds of thousands of carloads of oranges, lemons, cantaloupes, honeydews, lettuce, peas, cauliflower, and celery were being shipped east in refrigerated cars. In the 1870s, the British firm of Thomas Fyffe began to use refrigerated ships to import bananas, mangoes, and other tropical fruits from the West Indies and the Canary Islands, off the coast of Morocco, to London, and a new sight was seen on the streets of the city: thousands of fruit salesmen known as costermongers, selling cheap, fresh fruit to the masses. In 1878, the first French refrigerated steamer, appropriately named the *Frigorifique*, arrived at Le Havre with more than 5,000 carcasses of frozen beef. Refrigerated ships made it possible for Europeans to trade with new beef-producing countries such as Argentina and Australia, and meat became a more common sight on the tables of the middle class. Argentina and Australia also had vast herds of sheep, which supplied England's textile mills with more than 50 million pounds (22.6 million kg) of wool every year and helped to complete the transition to an industrial economy.

Preserving Food

Great strides were also made in the preservation of food, which not only made it easier to transport, but made it available throughout most of the year, long after it was harvested. The prime mover here was the emperor Napoleon. Napoleon is reported to have said that "An army marches on its stomach," but in fact he often didn't follow his own dictum and provided only limited packed rations for his troops, commanding them to live off the countryside when the rations were used up. The English were disturbed but tolerant of Napoleon's conquests until he invaded Spain, cutting off the supply of their favorite fortified wines: port and sherry. The English sent an army to Spain commanded by Sir Arthur Wellesley, later the Duke of Wellington. By skillfully maneuvering to cut off the French from Spain's agricultural regions, Wellington starved them out of the country. When Napoleon invaded Russia in 1812, the Russian policy of "scorching the earth"—destroying the food resources in the path of the advancing French soldiers—prevented them from living off the land. On the retreat from Moscow, the Grand Army, 600,000 men strong when it had invaded Poland, was reduced to no more than 10,000 troops.

Though he managed the matter poorly, food was always on Napoleon's mind. He offered a prize of 12,000 francs to anyone who could devise a new method of food preservation. The winner was the Parisian baker and confectioner Nicolas Appert, who placed food in glass bottles, boiled the bottles in water, and sealed the bottles with waxed corks while they were still boiling. The bacteria in the food were killed, and the food remained edible indefinitely. Unfortunately for Napoleon, this method of preservation was not practical for marching armies. The glass bottles were fragile and broke easily, and even a tiny undetectable crack could cause the food to spoil. But it was a step in the right direction, and in 1810 Appert published his treatise, *A Book for All Housekeepers: The Art of Preserving All Kinds of Animal and Vegetable Substances for Several Years*, and this set others on the search for a more practical solution.

By 1812, British inventor Bryan Donkin had learned how to pack boiled food into unbreakable tin canisters and was selling tinned beef, mutton, vegetable stew, and soup to the British Army. Smoked and salted meat finally disappeared from the soldier's diet. The technique of canning was next applied to ships' stores of water. By 1856, the American Gail Borden was selling tins of evaporated, powdered milk, the only kind of milk that was safe to drink before pasteurization. By the second half of the nineteenth century, people could enjoy meat and vegetables and fruit out of season, no matter where they lived.

Technology and Urbanization

The twentieth century witnessed another agricultural revolution with the invention of the gasoline engine. Now the farmer could pull his planters and harvesters across the fields with tractors or use a self-propelled "combine" to do the job. The horse, once the farmer's most important and reliable helpmate—itself requiring a good deal of fodder and care—all but disappeared from agriculture. From petroleum, scientists derived artificial fertilizers, and pesticides that reduced losses to crop-eating insects. Agricultural scientists devised new hybrid seeds that produced higher yields of grain. Mechanization eliminated much of the backbreaking labor of farming, increased output, and created a new food-production system frequently referred to as "industrial" agriculture. Gasoline became a farmer's greatest expense.

It was truly a new world, a world of bustling cities and sprawling urban areas, their skies darkened by the smoke of factories, and their people crowded into rows of drab tenements. But there was power in the cities, the power of accumulated money, and an incredible variety of foods could be found for sale in markets and shops. In addition to being able to shop at produce markets, butchers, bakers, and a variety of specialized food shops, a new middle class could now eat at restaurants, where owners competed for patrons by perfecting new recipes and gourmet dishes. People began to do something extraordinary, to go outside the home to eat, and the street life of the cities became colorful and exciting.

Paris led the world in fine dining and gourmet food preparation. The word "restaurant" means restorative, and that was what was on the sign of the first public dining shop that opened in Paris in 1765, selling soups and broths as a quick energy boost to customers. The name quickly caught on. In 1782, Antoine Beauvilliers opened the first luxury restaurant, La Grande Taverne de Londres. Anthelme Brillat-Savarin enjoys the distinction of being the first restaurant critic. After the French Revolution of 1789, the

The combine was invented for harvesting crops and virtually replaced the horse on most farms.

great aristocrats lost much of their property, and many chefs from the great houses were thrown out of work, only to prosper as restaurant owners in the cities. Over the next 100 years, the culinary experiments of chefs did more to change our tastes and preferences in eating than every previous revolution in food production or preparation. Some chefs became world famous. Georges-Auguste Escoffier, who made his reputation at the Savoy and Carlton Hotels in London, was called the "king of chefs and the chef of kings." Lorenzo Delmonico came to the United States in the 1830s and opened what was then the largest restaurant in the country in New York City. He introduced many new European dishes and popularized the restaurant and the idea of dining out in America.

The food of the cities came from all around the world. By the nineteenth century, the mercantile kingdoms of sixteenth- and seventeenth-century Europe had become powerful nation-states ruled by an alliance of old wealth and new commercial interests, backed up by the power of industrial mass production to equip large armies and navies. Building on the tradition of their earlier predatory explorations in search of spices and slaves, these nations marched into Africa, Asia, and Latin America to take control of the raw materials and cheap labor available there. It was the age of imperialism. Spain had penetrated vast regions of Central and South America as early as the sixteenth century. Great Britain established colonies in India, the Middle East, and western and southern Africa. Portugal conquered Brazil, Angola, and Mozambique. France took over the economies of North Africa and Indochina. Italy controlled Libya and parts of Somalia. Germany took Cameroon, Namibia, and Tanzania. Belgium conquered the Congo, and the Netherlands took Indonesia. By 1914, more than 80 percent of the land surface of the Earth was controlled by the Europeans, and even where there was no direct political control, as in China, nations lived under the constant threat of European naval power and were forced to adapt their trade policies to European interests.

The subject nations watched as their economies were converted from dependence on barter to cash, from food self-sufficiency to dependence on the income from crops grown for export, and from reliance upon a workforce of independent farmers to one of landless, low-wage laborers working on European-owned plantations and mines, and for other companies engaged in resource extraction. Europe's Industrial Revolution and its new legions of factory workers were ultimately sustained by cheap food from the subject nations. The agrarian economies of Africa, Asia, and Latin America had become dependent on the export of raw materials and agricultural products desired by the consumers of the developed countries. The legacy of colonialism has been a deep and conflict-ridden global division between rich and poor nations—between industrialized nation-states whose technology and manufactures make them the envy of the world, and poor agrarian societies whose struggles for national unity, modernization and development, and food self-sufficiency were blocked for more than 200 years.

Commercial Farming

Subsistence farming would persist into modern times, but more and more farmers all around the world were now growing food for sale in the marketplace. Food was becoming a commodity, grown to exchange for cash, and agriculture was becoming a branch of commerce. In the new world order, farmers were now part of a cash economy, and they had to grow money rather than food. Farmers were increasingly at the mercy of the marketplace, and their own higher productivity drove down the prices they received for their harvests. Increased production had made agriculture a seller's market, where prices were controlled by international traders, market speculators, shippers, wholesalers, processors, packagers, and the many other middlemen who took possession of the food after it left the farmer's hands. Farmers were also becoming increasingly dependent on the manufacturers of farm machinery, seed companies, and the petroleum companies.

By the mid-twentieth century, millions of small farmers in the indus-

In the twentieth century, farming became big business.

trialized nations had gone bankrupt and had been replaced by larger commercial farms organized like businesses, which had to produce enough cash income to cover the costs of the new agricultural technology. In the United States alone, from the Great Depression of the 1930s to the farm crisis of the mid-1980s, the number of people living on farms decreased from about 25 million to 5 million, as smaller, inefficient farms gave way to the commerical ones. Most of the farms were still family-owned, but it was the largest commercial operations that produced most of the food supply. A farmer could no longer survive simply because he produced enough food to feed himself. To keep his farm, he had to produce and sell enough surplus food to make payments on his land, tractors and combines, the fuel to run them, the fertilizers that made his land so productive, and the pesticides that protected his crops from insects. Farming was not simply a business; it was a big business. The average, successful, commercial grain farmer in the United States today has a capital investment in his farm of $1 million.

The same process of commercialization and land concentration reached into underdeveloped countries. Here, even into modern times, hundreds of millions of small farms continue to exist, but large-scale, plantation-style, export-oriented agriculture is increasingly dominant. Some of the plantation-style agricultural projects in the underdeveloped countries occupy areas of land the size of small countries. The farmers who worked such land when it existed as small plots, and who grew a variety of crops to feed themselves in a cashless society, began working for wages on the new, larger farms and producing only a few cash crops for export. Many left farming altogether, made redundant by farm mechanization and agricultural technology that reduced the need for labor, though in Third World nations there has been little industrializaion to employ the landless farmers. In the world of the new merchant-princes, farming had to show a profit like any other business. Farms existed principally to generate cash, not food, and they could make the most cash if they were large and worked by machinery and modern business methods that minimized the need for labor, even if this meant an assault on the way millions of traditional, small, self-sufficient farmers made their living.

Science, increasing world trade, urban wealth and political power, and the integration of free markets around the globe have transformed farming from a subsistence activity to an economic activity, and although farmers have thrown off the chains of feudalism, their new financial bonds to their creditors and suppliers have kept them at the lowest of society. Their lives are now regulated by the decisions made by bankers, merchants, shippers, packers, food processors, transnational corporations, and even financial speculators, all of whom view food as a commodity, like any other, to be sold or traded as profit. There is enormous pressure on farmers to use the latest agricultural technology in order to operate their farms as much as possible as industrial factories, to maximize output, and the cost of this technology bankrupts thousands of smaller farms every year and keeps thousands of other farms deeply in debt. Global food production has increased enormously, almost by 300 percent since the 1950s, but the same forces that have made this increase possible have also left a billion of the world's people impoverished and hungry. We will take a look at the problems of modern food production in the next two chapters.

Chapter Four
Food Production Today

In modern times, science, technology, and commerce have completely transformed the activities of farming, herding, and fishing. The primary producers—the farmer, the rancher, and the fisherman—are now only one small part of a vast network of people involved in food storage, transportation, processing, packaging, and marketing, as well as those involved in genetic research, agrochemistry, and the manufacture of farm machinery. In 1955, Harvard professor and former assistant secretary of agriculture John H. Davis coined the word *agribusiness* to describe this new system of food production. Though he was talking primarily about American agriculture, with the growth of world trade it is not inaccurate to talk about a global food-production system, in which almost all the nations, rich and poor, are linked through international markets and the activities of huge transnational marketing corporations and food-processing conglomerates. Many of the smallest, poorest, or most remote farmers, herders, and fishermen become part of this system either through dependence on suppliers of farm machinery, petrochemicals, seeds, and credit, or through the need to market their products to the middlemen who will transport, process, package, and sell their food to consumers around the world. Let's take a look at this food-production system, first in terms of what the world produces from agriculture, animal husbandry, and the harvest from the sea.

The world's fisheries are our least important source of food, though their contribution is hardly insignificant. On average, people obtain about 20 percent of their animal protein from the sea, though in some island nations and the coastal countries of Asia, that figure may be as high as 90 percent. We also receive an additional 5 percent of our animal protein from fish meal added to livestock feed. Fish also contain small amounts of vitamin A and B, calcium, iron, and iodine. There are more than 200 species of edible fish, but only about 40 species of marine animals are used in large quantities for food, and they fall into four categories: dermersal, or bottom-dwelling fish; pelagic, or surface-dwelling fish; crustaceans, or shellfish; and cephalopods and mollusks. Dermersal fish include haddock, cod, and sole. Pelagic fish include tuna, mackerel, herring, sardines, and anchovies. Crustaceans include lobster, crab, shrimp, scallops, and krill. And cephalopods and mollusks include squid, octopus, oysters, mussels, and clams. In addition to marine animals, many species of seaweed and algae are harvested for food. The Japanese eat seaweed for breakfast, and the Irish harvest an algae called carrageen, or "Irish moss." Fish, incidentally, are the only major human food source that still come from the wild.

Most of the world's important fisheries lie along the coastal waters of the continents, within 200 miles (320 km) of the shore. Some of the more productive areas include the northeast Atlantic, between Greenland and England, which yields about 16 percent of the total marine harvest; the northwest Pacific and west central Pacific, off the eastern coast of Asia, which produce about 40 percent of the total, and the southeast Pacific, off the western coast of South America, which produces about 10 percent of the total. About 15 percent of the fish we eat come from freshwater rivers and lakes. The fishing industries of five countries—Japan, Russia, China, the United States, and Chile—account for half of the total marine harvest. There are about 20 million fishermen in the world today, and the lives of more than 200 million people around the world depend upon their activities.

Commercial Fishing

The commercial fishing industry today is a product of modern technology. The fishing fleets are assisted in finding fish by helicopters and sonar-equipped surface vessels. Some fishing trawlers are huge ships with their own facilities for freezing and canning their catch. Plastic drift nets of sophisticated design extend for more than 10 miles (16 km) from the ships that deploy them. Iceland has just developed a trawling net that is large enough to ensnare a dozen Boeing 747s. And, of course, the fishing fleets would be nowhere as efficient as they are without modern marine engines and an adequate supply of petroleum. All this technology has produced a two-fold increase in the size of the fishing fleets and a four-fold increase in the marine harvest from 1950 to 1970, from about 20 million tons (18 million mt) to almost 90 million tons (81.6 million mt) of fish every year. But the commercial fishing industry is beset by problems, and its future is uncertain. For one thing, the fishing industry is not economically efficient. Almost $125 billion are spent every year to sustain an industry that brings in only about $70 billion worth of fish, and the difference is made up by government subsidies. Much more serious is the problem of overharvesting and declining fish stocks. Taking so many fish from the sea not only depletes current stocks, but it destroys breeding stocks for the next generation of fish.

Since the 1970s, fish stocks in most of the world's major fisheries have been declining. In the Atlantic Ocean, the harvest of cod has declined from a high of 380,000 tons (345,000 mt) in 1970 to about 60,000 tons (55,000

Sardine fishing in Japan. Together with Russia, China, the United States, and Chile, Japan is one of five countries that produce half of the world's marine harvest.

mt) in 1996. The catch of Pacific bluefin tuna has declined by about 75 percent during the same period, and the herring catch in the North Sea has dropped from 4 million tons (3.6 million mt) to 1 million tons (907,000 mt). In the Black Sea, the catch has dropped from 1 million tons (907,000 mt) in the 1980s to less than 200,000 tons (181,400 mt) in the early 1990s. In the 1970s, anchovy stocks off the coast of Peru fell from 20 million tons (18 million mt) to 4 million tons (3.6 million mt) and have since only rebounded to about 8 million tons (7.2 million mt). The harvest of king crabs in Alaska collapsed in the 1960s, and the sardine catch in California went into decline as early as the 1950s. By the 1980s, more than 40 of the world's most valuable fisheries were suffering from declining stocks. Growing world population, improved technology, the demand for fish meal for commercial livestock feed, marine pollution, and greed and mismanagement have all contributed to this decline. In many countries, governments have imposed severe restrictions on the fishing industry in order to protect spawning grounds. Another consequence of declining stocks has been conflict between nations over fishing rights, such as the "cod wars" between the European countries fishing in the waters near Iceland, and the dispute over the Grand Banks fishing area between Canada, the United States, and Spain. During the early 1970s, trawlers from the former East Germany, Poland, and the former Soviet Union caused outrage by severely depleting fish stocks in U.S waters. In 1982, 159 nations signed the United Nations Convention on the Law of the Sea, giving individual countries control of waters within a 200-mile (320-km) limit of their coastlines, and it was hoped that this would reduce overharvesting. But a significant number of nations with large fishing fleets have not signed the treaty, and there has been little evidence in the years since that fish stocks are recovering.

One proposed solution to the declining ocean harvest has been to devote more resources to aquaculture, the controlled breeding and raising of fish in "fish farms," that is, inland pools of water or protected coastal areas. Fish farming was practiced by the ancient Egyptians and the Romans. Such fish may be harvested directly from their protected areas or raised to maturity and then released into the sea. Today 8 percent of the total marine harvest, about 21 million tons (19 million mt) of fish, are raised in this way. From long experience in their rice paddies, Asian nations have learned to raise carp in isolated pools, and Americans do the same with freshwater trout, catfish, and crawfish. The state of Idaho produces about 18 million pounds (8 million kg) of trout every year, most of which is returned to U.S. rivers to benefit anglers. France raises oysters in this way, Ecuador has its shrimp farms, Japan specializes in sea bream and yellowtail tuna, and Norway raises salmon in small pens.

Aquaculture, however, has its own set of problems. As with all animals raised in confined conditions, disease spreads more rapidly. Ireland's trout fisheries were destroyed by the larvae of sea lice that escaped from their salmon farms. Some fish refuse to reproduce in confined conditions. Furthermore, many inland fish farms are located in agricultural areas, and are easily contaminated by pesticides and other chemicals carried through the soil by water. The waste products produced by the fish themselves in a confined area can pollute underground aquifers. The most serious obstacle, however, to expanding aquaculture is that the fish still have to be fed, either with fish meal or cereal grains. To produce 1 pound (.4 kg) of fish in a fish farm requires several pounds of other fish as food. It has been estimated that to sustain our present level of fish consumption exclusively through fish farming would require an additional 4 million tons (3.6 million mt) of grain per year, and that grain would have to come off people's tables. This is not an economical trade-off. Fish farming in general is not very profitable except for a few varieties of the more expensive seafoods such as oysters, shrimp, and salmon. Aquaculture has the advantage of not requiring large amounts of petroleum, as do the far-ranging fishing fleets, but it is doubtful that it can ever completely replace those fleets. This forces upon us serious questions about how we are going to manage and sustain our ocean resources in the years to come.

Meat and Dairy Production

Far more important to the human diet than fish is meat, our major source of protein. We obtain meat from a global supply of about 10 billion cattle, pigs, chickens, sheep, goats, turkeys, geese, and ducks. Cattle also provide us with leather for clothing and shoes; sheep provide us with wool; and ducks and geese provide feathers for insulating cold-weather clothing and sleeping bags. Hunting is no longer a significant economic activity, and with the exception of a few primitive societies, it has become the province of sportsmen. Our food animals are all domesticated species, grazed on about 7.4 billion acres (3 billion ha) of pastureland or fed on cereal grains, mostly corn. Red meat consumption is declining as people become concerned about the amount of fat they consume, but consumption of leaner meats from poultry is increasing. Animals also provide us with dairy products—milk, cheese, cream, and butter—and eggs. Eggs are an excellent source of protein, as well as vitamins A and B, calcium, and iron, though in recent years there has been concern about their high cholesterol content, which is a causal factor in heart disease. This, plus a growing dependence on processed, instant breakfast foods, has caused a decline in egg consumption in recent years. The 1996 *Fact Book* of the U.S. Department of Agriculture reported that Americans consume every year 112 pounds (51 kg) of red meat, 63 pounds (28.6 kg) of chicken and turkey, 30 pounds (13.6 kg) of eggs, 25 pounds (11.3 kg) of milk, 26 pounds (11.8 kg) of cheese, 10 pounds (4.5 kg) of animal fat (butter, lard, and oils), and 8 pounds (3.6 kg) of fluid cream. Worldwide, in 1996, people consumed 56 million tons (51 million mt) of beef, 56 million tons (51 million mt) of poultry meat, 84 million tons (76 million mt) of pork, and 11 mil-

Cattle provide us with meat as well as leather for shoes and clothing.

lion tons (9.9 million mt) of sheep and goat meat. Total meat consumption was more than 211 million tons (191 million mt).

In the United States, the three most important varieties of beef cattle are the Angus, Hereford, and Durham, or Shorthorn, breeds. The Angus originated in Scotland and was first brought to the Kansas prairie in 1873. It can be identified by its solid black color. Herefords originated in Herefordshire, England, and were brought to the United States in 1817 by Kentucky politician Henry Clay. The Durham is also from England, and is colored in red and white patterns. In India and Asia, the water buffalo and the humpbacked zebu, or Brahman, sandy or reddish-brown in color, predominate. But religious beliefs, especially among the Hindus and Muslims, limit their use as a source of beef. There are many other species of beef cattle, including the Beefmaster, the Africander, found in South Africa and Australia, and hybrid oddities like the Beefalo, a cross between various species and the American bison. The Charolais originated in France, and the Simmental can be found in central Europe and Russia. The best beef comes from the male animal, which is castrated at a young age and is then known as a steer. If beef cattle are slaughtered at a very young age, their meat is known as veal, which is more tender and less fatty than beef. Though many cattle are still grazed on open land, increasingly they are taken to special feedlots and fattened on special formulas of feed grain and protein supplements. Since disease spreads more rapidly when cattle are confined in feedlots, the animals are injected with antibiotic drugs. Half of the antibiotics produced by the American pharmaceutical industry are used to protect farm animals from disease.

Dairy breeds include the Holstein, the Jersey, the Guernsey, and the Ayrshire, though throughout the world people also obtain milk from goats, donkeys, camels, and reindeer. The modern dairy industry in the industrialized nations has been radically transformed by science and commerce. Because milk spoils very quickly, dairy farms once were relatively small farms and had to be located close to consumers. In the nineteenth century, Louis Pasteur discovered that boiling milk would kill the bacteria in it and prevent spoilage, and at about the same time Gail Borden invented a condensed form of milk that was less likely to spoil. Then came the refrigerated railway car and, in the twentieth century, the refrigerated truck. As late as the 1940s in the United States, farmers did not transport their milk to markets more than 40 to 50 miles (64 to 80 km) away, and most milk was delivered by trucks right to the consumer's doorstep. A merchandising revolution in the 1950s created the chain supermarket, which often owned its own milking plants, and kept its milk in refrigerated bins right in the store. Since cows must be pregnant to give milk, milk production increased dramatically with the development of techniques of artificial insemination. Milking itself is no longer done by hand, but by milking machines with tubes and vacuum pumps. Most recently, the Food and Drug Administration has approved a new bovine growth hormone that stimulates increased milk production, and one cow may now produce more than 12,000 pounds (5,440 kg) of milk annually, depending on the breed. All this new technology has made dairy farming a more expensive operation, and the small dairy farmer, delivering his milk to a local market, is becoming a thing of the past. The number of commercial dairy farms in the United States has fallen from 600,000 in 1952 to a little more than 100,000 today. The new, larger dairy farms with their automated feeding and milking machines are so productive that the government has had to purchase 5 billion pounds (2.3 billion kg) of surplus milk and dairy products every year just to prevent the collapse of prices paid to the farmer.

The reason that beef has been an expensive luxury food throughout most of human history has to do with what scientists call "reproductive inefficiency." After birth, it takes about two years before a cow reaches maturity and is able to calve, and this means that the farmer has to invest a lot of time and a lot of feed raising the animal. By comparison, from birth, a pig takes only four months to become a 200-pound (90-kg) hog, ready for the butcher. The pig also fattens itself on refuse and silage—the remnants of harvested crops—and does not require that a portion of the harvest be set aside for its food. This makes it an inexpensive animal to raise in countries where there is no surplus grain, though in the industrialized countries pigs are fed almost exclusively on surplus grain. From the hind legs of the hog, we obtain ham, and from the back, breast, and flanks, after curing and smoking, we get bacon. The chicken can also be raised fairly quickly and is much less expensive than beef. It was the one animal that medieval peasants could afford to keep. Chicken varieties are divided into egg-layers and broilers. Many nations of the world have created unique chicken dishes that are closely identified with their cultures. The French have *coq-au-vin*, or chicken in wine; the Spanish have paella, chicken, sea food, and rice; the Italians have chicken cacciatore, chicken and tomato sauce; and the Mexicans have molé, chicken with tomatoes, chili peppers, and chocolate sauce.

Sheep are also quick to mature and inexpensive to raise. From young sheep we obtain lamb, and from older sheep we obtain a somewhat tougher meat—mutton. Lamb has also been the subject of much experimentation by cooks. The Russian dish shash-lik—marinated and roasted lamb served on a skewer—was originally served on a real sword. Shish-kebob, from Armenia, is very similar. Curried lamb, served with rice, is popular in India, and couscous, minced lamb served with millet and vegetables, comes from North Africa.

Meat production in the Western nations very dramatically demonstrates both the benefits and the problems of the new food-production system. Factory farming, as it is called, has made meat and dairy products widely available to the masses for the first time in history. But assembly-line techniques keep the animals in unnaturally confined conditions. The widespread use of antibiotics in animal feed increases the rate at which bacteria become resistant to these drugs. The United States Centers for Disease Control estimated that as many as 2 million people a year are infected with antibiotic-resistant salmonella from eating meat and dairy products. Veal calves are confined in narrow crates to prevent movement, so that their muscles will not develop fully and their meat will be tender, and their feed formulas are deficient in iron, inducing anemia, so that their flesh will have the pale color preferred by consumers. Pigs are kept in small battery cages in rooms without light so that they will fatten quickly. Large amounts of waste products accumulate under the cages in these confinement houses, polluting the nearby land, and disease spreads rapidly. More than 80 percent of the pigs bred in the United States have contracted pneumonia by the time they are slaughtered.

    Egg-laying chickens are kept in small cages holding no more than eight birds. Unable to establish their natural "pecking order," they become aggressive and injure each other. To control aggression, their beaks and toes are trimmed with a hot blade. Male chicks are useless for egg-laying, and when they hatch they are discarded in plastic trash bags, where they suffocate. More than 500,000 male chicks are thrown away in this manner every day. Broiler chickens are not kept in tiny cages because the cages bruise their flesh, and this would be unappealing to consumers. Nevertheless, they are raised in crowded conditions and must also have their beaks and toes cut to reduce fighting. A chemical derived from plants, xanthophyll, is added to their feed to give their skin the yellow color consumers prefer. Though chickens have a natural lifespan of fifteen to twenty years, modern factory-feeding methods take them from the hatchery to the slaughterhouse in seven weeks. Even if one is not particularly concerned with the suffering of animals, the modern factory-farming system for livestock raises many environmental and human health issues that must be addressed. Another point that must be raised is that these factory-like methods of livestock raising, with their high capital investment in climate-controlled buildings, advanced machinery, and synthetic feed additives, have removed animals from the farmer's barnyard and made animal husbandry the province of large businesses and food corporations.

A more general problem associated with meat production, in a world where food resources are limited, is the inefficiency of producing animal protein for human consumption. Animals must be fed before they reach maturity and can be eaten themselves, and the higher up we go on the food chain, the less we get for what we put in. It takes about 16 pounds (7.3 kg) of animal feed—cereal grains, soybeans, and fish meal—to produce 1 pound (.4 kg) of beef and 8 pounds (3.6 kg) of feed to produce 1 pound (.4 kg) of pork. In the United States, 80 percent of our corn crop is used to feed livestock, and, globally, 40 percent of the world's cereal grains are fed to animals. It takes about 2 acres (.8 ha) of land to grow the grain required to produce enough meat for the average adult person in an industrialized country, but there is less than 1 acre (.4 ha) of farmland per individual in the entire world. The 2,000 pounds (907) kg) of grain required to produce one American's annual supply of meat would feed five people in one of the less-developed nations, if eaten as grain instead of meat. The United States is unique in having enough grazing land, unsuitable for the growing of food crops, to produce all the beef we need, but in other parts of the world, the wealthier meat-eaters are in competition with the poorer plant-eaters for the available grain supply. "If the Chinese," writes Susan George in *How the Other Half Dies*, "who raise about four times as many pigs as the Americans, collectively went mad tomorrow and began to feed their pigs on grain as Americans do, there would be very little grain left in the world for humans anywhere."[1] The rich nations of the world can outbid the poor nations for grain sold on world markets, driving up the price and making the grain unavailable to the poor. Many Third World nations, whose own people are inadequately fed, export beef to the industrialized nations, where it is often used for pet food. Almost 50 percent of the beef produced in Central America is exported, mainly to the United States. The more meat some people eat, the less grain there is available to feed people who cannot afford to eat meat. The most savage indictment of this system of meat production came from René Dumont, who compared it to a kind of cannibalism: "By consuming meat, which wastes the grain that could have saved them, last year we ate the children of the Sahel, Ethiopia, and Bangladesh. And we continue to eat them with undiminished appetite."[2]

When other agricultural inputs are considered, we discover that it takes about 2,500 gallons (9.460 liters) of irrigation water to produce 1 pound (.4 kg) of steak, and 20,000 calories of fossil fuel, though that pound of steak yields only 500 calories of food energy. In the United States, farmers produce more than twice the amount of cereal grains that Americans are able to consume, creating huge agricultural surpluses. Farmers are driven to maximize production to cover the high costs of modern agricultural technology—farm machinery, petroleum, fertilizer, pesticide. Francis Moore Lappé, in her provocative book *Diet for a Small Planet*, notes that our agricultural system is "well designed to get rid of an abundance of grain created by a relentless push to increase production. Because hungry people throughout the world could not afford to buy that grain, it was fed to livestock to provide more meat to the already well-fed."[3] Lappé goes on to argue that beef production in the industrialized countries is driven by economic forces rather than real need, and that a diet based on cereal grains, legumes, lentils, and other vegetables would provide all the necessary protein human beings need much more cheaply and efficiently, and it would feed more people.

Legumes

Wherever meat has proved too expensive, people have learned to depend upon another group of high-protein foods, the legumes, more commonly known as pulses, beans, or peas. Legumes have almost twice the protein

Soybeans originated in Asia and now are used as an important source of protein worldwide.

content of cereal grains. Legumes and cereals eaten together can provide human beings with all the essential amino acids. Legumes also have the ability to "fix" atmospheric nitrogen in the soil, restoring its fertility, and are therefore important in crop-rotation schemes to keep the land productive. One of the most important legumes, with a protein content as high as 38 percent, is the soybean. The soybean originated in Asia, where it is turned into soy sauce, used as a flavoring in almost all oriental dishes, and processed into a nutritious white paste called tofu. It is also rich in oils that are used to make salad dressings, cooking oils, and margarine, and it is an important protein supplement for animal feed. In Asia, you can also purchase a soft drink made from soybeans, called vitasoy. Sixty million bottles of vitasoy are sold every year, though the drink is almost unknown in the West. The soybean was brought to the United States from China in the nineteenth century, but did not become an important crop until the early twentieth century, when the agricultural scientist George Washington Carver proved that it could be adapted to the North American climate. The soybean has also proved to be a blessing for vegetarians, because its pulp can be spun into long fibers, combined with various food flavorings and coloring agents, and processed into look-alike and, in some people's opinions, taste-alike substitutes for various meats. So important has the soybean become to the American farmer and consumer that the United States, with an annual production of more than a billion bushels, is now the world's top grower of soybeans, outproducing China. Other important legumes are the peanut, also popularized by George Washington Carver, and the common pea, the chickpea or garbanzo, the lima bean, and the kidney bean.

Starchy Staples

Another important group of foods, though its members are not botanically related to each other, is commonly known as the starchy staples. This group includes the potato, the sweet potato, the banana, the yam, and manioc. These plants do not reproduce with seeds but instead by a process known as vegetative propagation. New plants grow out of a thickened stem or root known as a tuber, a kind of food sack, usually located in the ground. They are high in carbohydrates and provide some small amounts of vitamins, minerals, and protein. By far the most important of these plants is the potato, which in the past was often the main food of the poor. Russia is one of the world's largest producers of potatoes, with an annual crop of close to 100 million tons (90.7 million mt), and the average Russian eats more than 1 pound (.4 kg) of potatoes every day. The Irishman used to eat as much as 8 pounds (3.6 kg) a day. China, Poland, and Germany are also important potato-growing countries. Roots and tubers are staple foods for more than 1 billion people.

The Cereal Grains

Fish, meat, legumes, and starchy staples are important, but it is the cereal grains—wheat, rice, corn, millet, sorghum, oats, barley, and rye—that feed the world. This has been the case since biblical times, when the prophet Isaiah wrote that "all flesh is grass." Cereal grains provide the world's peoples with 51 percent of their energy intake. They are the staple foods of more than 4 billion human beings. In 1996, according to the Food and Agriculture Organization of the United Nations, the farmers of the world produced 1.8 billion tons (1.6 billion mt) of cereal grains. The most abundant crop is wheat, with more than 570 million tons (517 million mt) produced in 1996. There are many kinds of wheat, classified according to botanical characteristics and habits of growth. Hard red spring, hard red winter, and hard white wheat are most commonly used for breads; soft red winter and soft white wheat are used for baked goods such as cakes, biscuits, and pastries; durum, red durum, and amber durum are used to make noodles, spaghetti, and macaroni. If the entire wheat kernel is used in milling, including the germ and the bran, the result is a yellowish flour that produces whole-wheat breads. If the germ and the bran are removed before milling, the result is a less nutritious white flour. White flour is preferred for its superior baking qualities, but it must have vitamin and mineral additives to restore its value as a food. Wheat is the most important food commodity traded in international markets, and it is the cereal grain most often provided as food aid to developing countries, with the United States being the major supplier.

We have already mentioned the two major varieties of rice—*japonica* and *indica*. Though wheat is produced in greater quantities, rice actually feeds more people. About 90 percent of the world's rice crop is produced in Asia. Brown rice with its intact layer of bran is more nutritious, but people seem to prefer the less nourishing white rice, in which the bran layer is polished away. Rice can also be fermented to produce a wine called sake, which is popular in Japan. Rice is the staple food for almost half of the human race. Rice is a difficult commodity to trade on international markets because of consumer preferences. The Japanese and the South Koreans prefer *indica*, while the Europeans prefer *japonica*. In Bangladesh, people like their rice steamed and dehusked; in Senegal, it must be milled; and people in Jordan want it treated with paraffin oil. As a result, most of the rice crop is consumed in the countries where it is grown. Less than 5 percent of the world's rice crop leaves its country of origin.

There are actually hundreds of varieties of corn. Sweet corn is the variety offered to consumers in the fresh-produce departments of groceries and supermarkets. Its sugars are slow to turn into starch after harvesting, so it retains its sweetness for a longer time than other varieties do. Some varieties of sweet corn stay sweet for as long as ten days after harvesting if properly refrigerated. Popcorn contains a tough starch-protein layer within the kernel, so that when the kernel is heated and the moisture inside it turns to steam, that steam is not immediately released, but builds up pressure within the kernel until the grain literally explodes and turns itself inside out. In 1893, Charles Cretors of Chicago invented a popcorn steamer that could be carried on a street wagon, and popcorn became popular among the urban masses. A few years later, Frederick William Ruckheim and his brother Louis, also from Chicago, began to sell bins of a new kind of popcorn sweetened with molasses. At the turn of the century, Henry Eckstein joined the Ruckheim brothers and developed a moisture-proof cardboard box so that the popcorn could be more widely marketed in smaller quantities. After the naval battle of Jutland in 1916, the Ruckheims adorned the box with a picture of Frederick's grandson, dressed in a sailor suit, along with his pet dog Bingo. They put small prizes inside the box, and named it Cracker Jack. In the 1960s, an agricultural extension agent from Indiana by the name of Orville Redenbacher developed a hybrid popcorn with "higher popping volume" and marketed it with his own face on the label, and today that face is familiar to millions of Americans.

There is also dent corn, flint corn, and flour corn. In the United States, most of the corn crop, more than 80 percent of it, is used as livestock feed, yet it is such a versatile product that many Americans would be surprised to learn that they consume about 3 pounds (1.4 kg) of corn per person per day. Much of this is in the form of corn starch, corn oil, and corn syrup used in processed foods, but even that doesn't tell the whole story. Corn by-products can be found in toothpaste, lipstick, shoe polish, bourbon, laundry detergents, synthetic fibers, paper products, rubber products, antibiotics, glues, plastics, explosives, aluminum, and even embalming fluid.

The Green Revolution

The cereal grains also dramatically illustrate the power of modern science to enhance our ability to produce food. Farmers have been selectively breeding grains for higher yields since the beginnings of agriculture, but it is very difficult to maintain pure strains of food plants grown in open fields, because they are exposed to whatever types of pollen are carried on the wind. Beginning in the 1920s, entrepreneurs and plant geneticists began to take an interest in this process by crossbreeding various strains of food plants in the laboratory. The first breakthrough came in 1926, when Henry A. Wallace, future secretary of agriculture under President Franklin Roosevelt and owner of the Pioneer Hi-Bred Corn Company, began marketing a variety of hybrid corn that increased farmers' yields by 25 percent. Forty years later, in the mid-1960s, more than 95 percent of the corn produced in the United States was grown from hybrid seed. In the 1950s, the plant geneticist Dr. Norman Borlaug developed a hybrid wheat, which was known as dwarf wheat because its stalk was shorter than the conventional wheats. Dwarf wheat converted the nutrients it absorbed into a larger head of grain rather than a tall stalk, and it could quadruple farmers' output. The short, tough stalk responded better to heavy doses of fertilizer and was also easier for mechanical harvesters to gather. It was developed in response to food shortages in the underdeveloped countries and widely planted in places such as Mexico and India. It boosted agricultural production enormously, initiating what has been called the Green Revolution.

In 1962, the Ford Foundation and the Rockefeller Foundation teamed up to establish the International Rice Research Institute (IRRI) in the Philippines, and in a short time the IRRI had developed a more productive dwarf rice, known as IR8. Other hybrid strains of cereal grains followed, until the development of hybrid seeds became a separate industry. Between 1950 and 1984, the hybrid seeds of the Green Revolution resulted in a 260 percent increase in global grain production. Between 1967 and 1982, wheat production in India increased by 300 percent, and between 1960 and 1980, rice production in the Philippines increased by 200 percent. Per capita output, the amount of available grain for each individual, increased by 80 percent in China. In Western Europe, where population growth was slower, per capita output increased by 130 percent.

In recent years, agricultural scientists have gone from simply crossbreeding existing seeds to actually manipulating the genes within those seeds and producing new plant varieties by creating new DNA. In 1994, the United States Food and Drug Administration approved the first genetically altered food plant for sale to consumers: a tomato called the Flavr Savr created by the Calgene company of Davis, California. Calgene scientists altered a gene inside the tomato seed that produced an enzyme that made the tomato rot. The new tomato stays fresher for a longer time on supermarket shelves, and consumers, who purchase $4 billion worth of tomatoes every year, can now hope to purchase a tomato with a garden-fresh taste, instead of the pulpy, tasteless tomatoes that are often sold out-of-season. The gene splicers are now on the march. The Monsanto and Frito-Lay Corporations are developing a starchier potato that absorbs less cooking oil and which will lead to less greasy French fries. The Upjohn Company is working on virus-resistant cantaloupes and squash, and Louisiana State University is involved in creating a rice kernel with an increased protein content. Other projects may produce pineapples that ripen more uniformly, corn that requires less protection from pesticides, and coffee beans with less caffeine.

The Green Revolution increased world agricultural output, but it also radically changed the way farmers work. In the past, the farmer would take a portion of his harvested grain and set it aside as seed for next season's planting. The new hybrid seeds were the products of the companies and research laboratories that developed them, and the farmer could not simply purchase them on a one-time basis and keep growing them because wind-borne pollen from other plants would "corrupt" them in the open fields. Now the farmer had to go back to the seed companies every year and purchase more hybrid seed. Seed became a new commercial input that the farmer had to pay for, rather than grow himself. Furthermore, selectively bred for higher yields, the new hybrids sacrificed some of their hardiness and resistance to disease. The popularity of hybrid seeds led to increasing dependence on monoculture, with vast regions planted with one species of high-yielding cereal grain. Species diversity and crop variety make it difficult for plant blights and insect pests to find their favorite foods, but monoculture makes the harvests more vulnerable. Many of the new hybrid seeds last only a few years before their natural predators adapt and ravage the crops grown from them. Researchers must continually create new varieties and sell them to farmers. The International Rice Research Institute in the Philippines maintains a stock of more than 80,000 varieties of rice for this purpose. The new hybrids also require greater inputs of fertilizer, pesticide, and fungicide to thrive. These too were products that the farmer had to purchase from agrochemical companies. So while yields increased, the farmer became more deeply enmeshed in the new system of industrial agriculture. How much more efficient the new hybrids were is subject to debate, considering the increased costs of petroleum-based products the farmer had to buy to sustain them. This became evident in the early 1970s, when the Organization of Petroleum Exporting Countries (OPEC) drastically raised the price of oil, and the price of fertilizers rose by 600 percent.

The effects of the Green Revolution were not entirely positive for this reason. It seems to be a general rule that, wherever there are pre-existing disparities in wealth, power, or access to economic resources, the introduction of new technology only exacerbates, or increases, those disparities. Hybrid seeds and the chemicals they required made farming more expensive, as had happened earlier with the introduction of new farm machinery, and only the wealthier farmers could take advantage of the new agricultural technology. The Green Revolution drove many poorer farmers deeply into debt and ruined them, while the larger commercial farms received most of the economic benefits. The Green Revolution has contributed to the increasing concentration of land ownership in the hands of a smaller number of better-off farmers, and it has made the farmers of many underdeveloped nations more dependent on the advanced technology of the industrialized nations. In her harsh indictment of the Green Revolution in *Ill Fares the Land*, Susan George writes that "This revolution was, in fact, an alternative to agrarian reform, which implies redistribution of power: it was a means of increasing food production without upsetting entrenched interests (as well as a means of providing increased revenues to the Western firms supplying industrial inputs)."[4] Dependence on advanced Western agricultural technology has contributed to a debt crisis and an unfavorable balance of trade in Third World nations, a problem that we will look at more fully in the next chapter, which seeks to examine why, in a world where biotechnology has vastly increased agricultural output, there is still widespread hunger and malnutrition.

Food Production

Who controls the production of food has been one of the central themes of this book, so before we take a look at the problem of hunger we should examine the role of the new merchant-princes—the transnational corporations and food conglomerates—and how they distribute the world's food supply. The production of many agricultural products is localized. That is, more wheat is grown in North America than can be grown in Africa, many exotic fruits and vegetables must be imported from the tropics, and some countries such as the island nations of Japan and Britain simply lack the land to grow all the food they need. To provide a varied and adequate diet for the world's peoples, therefore, farmers must rely on international traders, rail and shipping companies, and the banks and currency traders who support them. Even when food is consumed within its country of origin, farmers can no longer do without a complex assortment of food

Many foods in supermarkets have been chemically changed and supplemented with artificial flavorings and preservatives.

Soft drinks and other bottled beverages often seem to replace simple water.

processors and packagers, for in the modern world consumers have chosen to spend less of their time selecting and preparing what they eat, and have come to depend on what are called convenience foods. In the United States, for example, more than half of the food we eat is first altered by about 22,000 food-processing companies. Farm-fresh products are mechanically and chemically changed and supplemented with artificial flavorings, food colorings, sweeteners, preservatives, and additional nutrients, and packed into cans, bottles, and boxes, all so that food storage and cooking will be less of a chore for individual households. Cereal grains come to us in the form of packaged bakery products and instant breakfast foods. More than half of all the potatoes we consume come to us in the form of potato chips, frozen French fries, and instant mashed potatoes. Our fruits are converted into jellies and jams, snack foods, and candies. Some of us have even forgotten how to drink water, and depend for essential fluids on sodas, fruit drinks, and bottled beverages. Before the invention of the home refrigerator, people went to the market every day to pick fresh food for the day's meals. Now we prowl the aisles of supermarkets, purchasing in bulk for the entire week. Our fresh farm products are hidden from us behind what Robert West Howard in his book *The Vanishing Land* has called "the plastic curtain."

The work of farmers has become almost insignificant in determining the total price of our food products. Farmers receive no more than 25 percent of the retail price of processed foods, the rest going to the shipper, the processor, the packager, and the advertiser. The farmer in Sri Lanka receives no more than 20 percent of the retail price of a packet of his tea sold in England. The cost of corn in a box of breakfast cereal amounts to no more than 5 percent of what the consumer pays for it. In the early 1980s, for example, the American national food bill was about $300 billion, but American farmers received only about $85 billion for their efforts. Looked at another way, the cost of convenience foods for the consumer is four times the value of the food itself, as a large number of profit-motivated businesses and food-processing firms have interposed themselves between the farmer and the consumer. This makes it harder for the farmer to bargain effectively for a fair price for his crops, and as the cost of land, machinery, seed, fertilizers, pesticides, and bank credit goes up, the farmer is caught is what is known as the "cost-price squeeze." This has made many small farms debt-ridden, unprofitable operations, and in many of the industrialized nations governments have had to subsidize these smaller farms to prevent them from going out of business. For more than 60 years, the American government has, through a system of loans, payments, and guaranteed price supports, tried to keep the small farmer from losing his land, and similar systems are in place in many of the industrialized countries. In fact, when nations get together to talk about establishing open markets and freer trade, government subsidies to farmers are one of the major sticking points in reaching agreements. It was only in 1996, in keeping with the spirit of the General Agreement on Tariffs and Trade (GATT) and the North American Free Trade Agreement (NAFTA), that the U.S. Congress passed a new farm bill designed to eliminate these subsidies in seven years. Perhaps a million small farms in the United States will then disappear.

In underdeveloped countries, such government protection is rare, and every year tens of thousands of small farmers simply give up, sell their farms, and join the legions of landless and unemployed people who no longer have the means to feed themselves. There are more than 1 billion farmers in the world, and only about 50 million of them live in countries where agriculture is highly mechanized and directly dominated by the agribusiness system. The vast majority of the world's farms are small, family-owned plots located in the developing countries, producing food mainly for the family-owners. But the rising cost of farming is gradually turning even these farms into commercial operations growing cash crops, and not everyone survives the uncertainties of commercial farming. In 1994, there were 500 million landless people in the rural areas of underdeveloped countries and another 400 million without enough land to make commercial farming work. The transition to commercial export farming also removes land from local food production, so that less food is sold locally at a higher price, creating food shortages and forcing a greater dependence on imported foods.

The Transnationals

Who are the agribusiness firms that control our food supply and the fate of so many of its producers? Let's briefly profile some of the companies involved in one area of food production—the most important one—cereal grains. Six large transnational grain-trading companies control most of the world trade in grain. Some of them, because they are privately owned, do not report their earnings to market regulatory commissions and operate in great secrecy. One of them, Cargill, Inc., is the largest privately held corporation in the United States. Cargill is, in fact, the world's largest trader of grain, with 1,600 factories and offices in 66 countries and sales of more than $5 billion. The Cargill brothers started buying grain elevators in Iowa shortly after the Civil War, and working with the railroads, they were able to monopolize the transport of grain to eastern cities. After the Depression, the companies' successors added a fleet of barges to their holdings to help transport the grain, and eventually entered the shipping industry as well, helping to build ships for the U.S. Navy during World War II. Today, the company is involved in the marketing of grain and oilseeds, coffee and cocoa, molasses and sugar, beef and pork, corn sweeteners, ethanol, cotton, rubber, and fruit concentrates, not to mention its steel, petrochemical, and life insurance businesses. It has recently announced its intentions to build storage elevators in Bolivia, animal feed and glucose syrup plants in Poland, a sunflower processing plant in the Ukraine, and a soybean-processing plant in Mexico. Cargill handles one-quarter of all U.S. grain exports, and when the United States lends money to other nations to buy American grain, a good portion of that money comes back to Cargill.

One of Cargill's competitors is the Continental Grain Company. It was founded in Belgium in 1813 by Simon Fribourg. During the Depression, the Fribourgs started to buy up American grain elevators, and when the Nazis invaded Belgium in 1940, they moved their business headquarters to New York City and renamed the company Continental. Today they are involved in the trade of corn, rice, and other grains, as well as cotton, soybeans, and pork and poultry. They own Allied Mills and Quaker Oats, and they have an interest in the Overseas Shipping Group, the nation's largest operator of ships for the transport of food commodities. The Fribourgs' personal fortune has been estimated at more than $1 billion. In 1994, citizens in Missouri, afraid of possible soil and air pollution, protested Continental's efforts to open pork-producing plants in the state.

Another major player in the grain trade is Archer-Daniels-Midland (ADM), "supermarket to the world." In 1878, John Daniels started a linseed oil-processing business in Minneapolis. George Archer, another linseed processor, joined the firm in 1903. The company purchased Midland Linseed Products in 1923 and took its present name. Since that time it has acquired many companies, including Fleishmann Malting, Corn Sweeteners, Supreme Sugar, Collingwood Grain, Ogilvie Mills, Pfizer Citric Acid, and Colombian Peanut, the latter purchase making it the largest domestic sheller of peanuts. ADM is the world's largest miller of corn and is also involved in the processing of cooking oils, amino acids, xanthum gum, and monosodium glutamate. It owns 200 factories that process 150,000 tons (136,080 mt) of grain and vegetable products every day. In the late 1960s, the company pioneered the development of textured vegetable protein from soybeans. Since the mid-1990s, ADM has been under investigation by the Justice Department and the Federal Bureau of Investigation for the alleged price-fixing of lysine, citric acid, and corn syrup. ADM also makes large contributions to both political parties in the United States in its efforts to promote the use of ethanol, an alcohol produced from corn, in gasoline.

Chiquita Brands International, Inc., though not involved specifically in the grain trade, must be mentioned because of its long history as a dominant force in Latin American agriculture. It was founded, as we have seen, by Lorenzo Baker, who began shipping Jamaican bananas to the United States in 1870. When the Boston produce-trader Andrew Preston joined the firm in 1885, it became the Boston Fruit Company. In 1899, Boston merged with three other fruit companies to become the United Fruit Company, and it soon owned vast plantations and warehouses throughout Latin America. It was purchased by Eli Black in 1970 and became United Brands and finally became Chiquita Brands International in 1990. As United Fruit, the company was known in Central America as the "Octopus." It established an alliance with the wealthy Honduran fruit grower Samuel Zemurray, who in 1905 engineered the overthrow of the Honduran government to achieve policies that were more favorable to the banana business. When the government of Guatemalan president Jacobo Arbenz tried to nationalize United Fruit holdings in 1954, the company convinced Congress that Arbenz was a communist, and United Fruit provided the ships that transported the marines for Arbenz's overthrow. The young Fidel Castro worked on a United Fruit sugar plantation, and the company also provided ships for the Cuban exiles who sought to overthrow him during the Bay of Pigs invasion in 1961.

Today, competition from Dole and restrictions on banana imports to the countries of the European Union are forcing Chiquita to streamline its business and sell off unprofitable operations. In February 1996, the company began evicting small growers from its Tacmiche plantation in Honduras, using government police and army troops to do so. United Fruit had acquired 3,000 acres (1,214 ha) of Honduran land in the 1920s for the sum of $1, but it now claims that the land is not profitable for banana growing. The 1,200 or so people that were evicted are fighting back with the help of local Catholic priests. Though these small growers, who earned about $3 a day working for Chiquita, could easily grow food on this land and support themselves, it has instead been sold to other companies who have planted it with corn and soybeans for the lucrative livestock-feed market.

There are hundreds of other food-processing and marketing corporations that are perhaps not so big but demonstrate the way in which integration and diversification give agribusiness such enormous economic power. The Sara Lee Corporation of Chicago is best known for its frozen baked goods. Its trademark product was cheesecake. But today the company makes about half of its income from apparel and personal care products. It owns the L'eggs hosiery company and the Hanes underwear company, as well as selling Brylcream and Endust. It controls the Playtex and Wonderbra companies, and in the 1990s it acquired a cosmetics company in Uruguay, a coffee company in Greece, and a pork producer in France. The Ralston Purina Company began in the 1890s by selling a new wheat cereal called Purina, but it is now the leading producer of cat and dog foods, cat litter, soy protein, baby foods under the Beech-Nut label, and with the acquisition of the Eveready and Energizer brands, the number-one producer of dry cell batteries.

Tyson Foods, whose owner Don Tyson was a big contributor to Bill Clinton's campaign for the Arkansas governorship, exports chickens to more than 40 countries and controls 53 percent of chicken exports in the United States. It became a company of more than $1 billion in sales in the 1980s, when health-conscious consumers began to turn away from red meat in favor of poultry. But today the company is also involved in egg production, livestock feed, beef, pork and, since its acquisition of Arctic Alaska Fisheries in 1992, seafood. Diversification enables a company to absorb losses from unprofitable operations and channel capital to those divisions that are more profitable. A strike by farmworkers for higher wages, a new tax by a foreign government, the rising cost of some raw material, a consumer boycott or loss of interest in one food, hardly fazes such food conglomerates. They can become almost invulnerable to the fickleness of the marketplace, and they can buy or sell all around the world to manipulate prices and maximize profits, regardless of the consequences to producers or consumers. This is real economic power, power over the global marketplace.

Falling Prices

The growing worldwide trend of selling crops for cash puts small farmers in underdeveloped countries at the mercy of the global marketplace and the agribusiness system, even if their activities hardly resemble those of farmers in the industrialized nations. The prices they receive for their harvests are determined by the output of competing producers, and many Third World nations, as a result of colonial policy, produce the same small variety of food crops. Sixty underdeveloped countries, for example, compete with each other for the world coffee market. The economy of Madagascar, which thought it had cornered the world market for vanilla, was nearly destroyed when Indonesia began to market a cheaper product. The anchovy fisheries of Peru, which collapsed in the early 1970s, will probably never recover their former prosperity because of the growth of the soybean industry in the United States, since soybeans compete favorably with fish meal as a protein supplement. With a global surplus of food engendered by the revolution in agricultural technology, prices for farm products are driven to new lows, making farmers in poor countries especially vulnerable to the market manipulations of the transnationals. The price of a 130-pound (59-kg) sack of coffee beans sank from more than $300 in 1977 to less than $80 in 1993. Between 1982 and 1992, the price of 2 pounds (.9 kg) of cocoa fell by 60 percent. And as the prices of manufactured goods in the industrialized nations rise, the value of raw agricultural materials falls by comparison, and the food exports of underdeveloped nations buy fewer and fewer Western goods.

The important point to remember, in a global cash economy and a world where food is traded as a commodity, is that the farmer's prosperity and survival does not depend on the amount of food that he or she grows but on the price received for that food and the cash income that the farmer obtains for selling it. When the poorer nations, which have few industrial products to sell, compete with each other to sell the same agricultural products, they drive down prices on international markets and make their food exports less valuable, less able to be exchanged for the other products these nations need, and economic development is made more difficult. Advanced agricultural technology increases yields, further driving down prices, though it makes farming more expensive. All this has contributed to increasing poverty and hunger among the farmers of underdeveloped nations, even as they have worked to increase the global food supply.

Everything else has changed in the world of the new merchant-princes and the transnational corporations, but one thing has not changed: the position of the farmer at the bottom of the economic and social ladder. The farmer remains one of the hardest-working, most poorly rewarded, least empowered, and hungriest members of civilization. It is now appropriate to turn to what is clearly the most pressing food problem facing us today, in spite of the enormous increase in agricultural output: the persistence of widespread hunger throughout the world. We will see how the global food production system and the institutions that control it are closely connected to the question of who eats and who goes hungry.

Chapter Five
Hunger

At the time that this book is being written, the world population is between 5.7 billion and 5.8 billion people, and it is increasing at the rate of 90 million people each year. Sometime shortly before the year 2000, there will be 6 billion people in the world. By various estimates, between 700 million and 1 billion of those people, as many as one in every six, will be malnourished. They will not receive enough food to maintain their health, and they will be slowly starving to death. The majority of them, ironically, perhaps 70 percent, will be farmers and landless agricultural workers, the people who produce our food. Between 400 million and 600 million of them will be children under the age of fifteen. More than 95 percent of these people live in the underdeveloped nations of Africa, Asia—more than 500 million in India alone—and Latin America, but in case anyone thinks that hunger is a distant problem, about 8 million adults and 12 million children in the United States are also malnourished. In spite of a global agricultural system that has nearly tripled its output of food in the last 50 years, between 40 million and

60 million people die of hunger and hunger-related diseases every year. Why is this so?

The two answers that first come to mind are really the same answer, opposite sides of the same coin, so to speak. There is not enough food, or there are too many people. This is a common answer given by many population experts. But does it make sense? We noted that in 1996 the world's farmers produced a total of more than 1.8 billion tons (1.6 billion mt) of cereal grains. With a current world population of 5.8 billion people, and assuming that no cereal grains are fed to livestock, that works out to about one-third ton (.3 mt), or more than 660 pounds (300 kg), of grain per person per year, or about 1.8 pounds (.8 kg) of grain per person per day. While 1.8 pounds (.8 kg) of grain a day will certainly not result in a lifestyle of gluttony, it will definitely prevent starvation, and we have not even considered supplementary sources of food such as fish, legumes, root crops, vegetables, and fruits.

It would seem that, if we were not competing for food with our domesticated animals, and if food were distributed equitably, the world can be fed. Curtis Skinner, writing in the journal *Social Policy* in 1988, noted that "the earth *presently* produces more than *twice* as much food as needed to provide all of its human inhabitants with a basic diet." Francis Moore Lappé and Joseph Collins, in their 1986 book *World Hunger: Twelve Myths*, write that "The world today produces enough grain to provide every human being on the planet with 3,600 calories a day." The Food and Agriculture Organization of the United Nations estimates that 2,200 calories a day will provide an adequate diet.

Lappé and Collins go on to write that *"Abundance, not scarcity, best describes the supply of food in the world today.* Rarely has the world seen such a glut of food looking for buyers. Increases in food production during the past 25 years have outstripped the world's unprecedented population growth by about 16 percent. Indeed, mountains of unsold grain on world markets have pushed prices downward over the past three decades."[1]

The World's Population

To be fair, however, food is not grown in all areas of the world, nor is it parceled out equally to the world's population. And neither are the world's peoples spread out evenly across the globe; they are not even distributed so as to have equal access to the 11 percent of the planet's land that is used for agricultural production. So isn't it still possible that locally, regionally, a large population might be putting too much pressure on the available food supply? Isn't that what population experts really mean when they talk about too many people? The rates of population growth in many underdeveloped nations are much higher than those of industrialized nations, and these seem to be the nations where there is insufficient food. But there are problems with this argument too.

The population density of the Netherlands is more than 1,000 people per square mile (2.5 sq km), and hunger is not a serious problem. The population density of Bolivia, on the other hand, is only 18 people per square mile (2.5 sq km), and there is widespread hunger. The population of Great Britain is more than 620 people per square mile (2.5 sq km), whereas the population of Brazil is only 50 people per square mile (2.5 sq km). The population density of many poor, agrarian countries in the Third World is lower than the population density of many of the smaller industrialized European countries, and yet there is more hunger in the countries where there are fewer people. India has twice the arable land that China has, and fewer people, and yet there is widespread hunger in India and relatively none in today's China. Crowded urban populations in industrialized nations generally feed themselves adequately in spite of having no local agricultural resources. They have not forgotten the lesson learned by the medieval burghers that the wealth of their manufactures can be exchanged for all the food they need. The industrialized nations, in the language of economists, have learned to ensure food security without food self-sufficiency. For these nations—and this is a critical point—trade with agrarian nations is essential for survival.

Between 40 million and 60 million people die of hunger or hunger-related diseases each year.

It is true that there are places in the world where vast populations are crowded along one river valley or into one river delta, completely dependent on an agricultural system plagued by floods and monsoons, as in Southeast Asia. And there are other places, such as the Sahel in Northern Africa, where large numbers of people are driven from the land and crowded together by the forces of drought and desertification. But there does not appear to be any simple correlation between the number of people in a region, the amount of farmland, and the adequacy of the food supply. As we shall see—and this has been true throughout the history of civilization—population and food supply are overshadowed as causes of abundance or hunger by industrial capacity, technological advantage, political and military power, systems of land tenure, divisions of wealth between classes and nations, and international economic power, as measured by the ability to influence prices in the marketplace. These factors have more to do with who eats than how crowded together we are or where our food comes from.

In spite of the fact that a single individual in the industrialized nations may use more than twelve times the food and energy resources of a person in an underdeveloped country, few experts argue for radical measures to control population in the industrialized world. Population control is primarily a policy aimed at the underdeveloped nations, where the experts perceive the higher birth rates as a threat to economic growth. Anne H. Ehrlich of Stanford University says that "rapid population growth quickly absorbs any gains made in economic development." In the history of Western industrialization, however, a rapidly growing population was essential to economic growth. A growing population provided the workers for the new factories and the markets for mass-produced goods. In the United States, massive immigration supplemented the natural birth rate. Why should a growing population suddenly become such a problem for this next generation of developing nations? Arguments that a large population hinders economic growth are Malthusian, based upon the ideas of the nineteenth-century English economist Thomas Malthus, who believed that people would multiply so fast that even industrialized societies would be unable to feed them all. But Malthus has been proved wrong. As Lappé and Collins indicate, the world's food supply has grown more rapidly than its population. Though few population experts would express it so crudely, there is something in their argument that harkens back to the England of Charles Dickens, where some people believed that if the poor would only stop breeding, there would be no hunger.

In truth, the poor do stop breeding—when they are no longer poor—and many population experts may have the relationship between high birth rates and hunger the wrong way around. In underdeveloped nations, a large family provides additional labor and income, insurance against high death rates from childhood diseases, and caring children for the elderly in societies without pensions and social security. In the more affluent industrialized nations, where there is greater financial security, especially in old age, the rate of population growth has been falling naturally without any mandatory birth-control policies. It would seem that hunger causes rapid population growth, and not the reverse. This is not to say that high population growth rates are not a problem for underdeveloped nations or that overpopulation won't become a serious concern for the entire world in the future. But to focus on population growth as the cause of hunger is to miss the point, and that point is that ever since the appearance of agriculture and civilization, our food production system has been characterized by food surpluses. And it is how we distribute food through our political and economic institutions that really determines who eats and who does not eat.

Wealth and Poverty

The cause of hunger, in a world where food is a commodity and cash is the medium of exchange, is poverty—that is, lack of an adequate source of income to purchase the basic necessities of life. The root cause of global hunger is the deep division between rich and poor nations, and the disparities of wealth between different groups of people within those nations, and that is the legacy of colonialism. The association between population density and hunger in various nations is unconvincing, yet the association between hunger and income levels is undeniable. The average annual per capita GNP, the amount of wealth per person, in the industrialized nations where there is the lowest incidence of hunger is about $13,000, and in countries such as Japan, Switzerland, and the United States, it is in excess of $20,000. The average annual per capita GNP in the developing nations, where hunger is concentrated, is about $700, and 35 of the most hungry nations in Africa and Asia, with a combined population of 2 billion people, have a per capita GNP of less than $400. These averages, of course, conceal enormous differences in wealth between different classes within the underdeveloped nations, for the majority of the people in these poorer countries actually subsist on incomes of less than $100 per year. And the gap between rich and poor nations is widening. Between 1965 and 1985, the industrialized nations increased the average annual income of their people by almost $4,000, whereas people in the underdeveloped nations increased their annual incomes by only $50 during the same period. In September 1998, the United Nations released its Human Development Report for that year and concluded that the richest 20 percent of people in the developed nations account for 80 percent of all private consumption, whereas the poorest 20 percent of people in underdeveloped nations consumed only 1.3 percent of the world's wealth. In Africa, the report stated, the average family actually consumes 20 percent less that it did twenty-five years ago.

And as one would expect in agrarian societies where land is wealth, there is also a correlation between hunger and the concentration of land ownership. In Central America, for example, depending on the country, between 35 percent and 70 percent of the population are malnourished. In El Salvador, 1 percent of the largest farms occupy more than 40 percent of the available farmland, and 60 percent of the rural population are landless. In Honduras, 4 percent of the largest farms occupy 56 percent of the available farmland, and 35 percent of the rural population are landless. In Latin America as a whole, 7 percent of the population controls 93 percent of the land. Concentration of land ownership is also a fact of life in other regions of the world, but we must change our perspective to understand it. In Southeast Asia, for example, the need to intensively manage and irrigate rice paddies keeps landholdings small, and unlike the huge latifundios and corporate plantations of South America, in Asia a farm of 25 to 100 acres (10 to 40 ha) would be considered the holding of a large and powerful landowner. Throughout the world, 80 percent of all farms are less than 12 acres (4.9 ha) in size. Most of the world's hungry are hungry because they are poor or because they are farmers who have no land to farm.

What forces have sustained and aggravated poverty and landlessness in the forty to forty-five years since the subject peoples of Africa, Asia, and Latin America won their political independence in the late 1950s and 1960s? Well, one might say that forty-five years is hardly time to recover from 200 years of colonial exploitation, and that is true. But, as we shall see, there are forces at work in the world today that have kept the basic economic relationship between rich and poor nations unchanged since colonial times. These forces include unfair trading relationships between the rich and poor nations, the virtual monopoly of the rich nations over industrial and agricultural technology, inequities in land ownership and access to economic resources, the absence of democratic institutions and processes in the poor nations, the development policies forced upon the poor nations by the rich nations, and the global transformation of agriculture from small-scale subsistence farming to large-scale commercial farming and the growing of cash crops for export. All of these forces are sustained by the activities of the agents of global commerce, the transnational corporations who produce and trade food for those who can pay for it.

For many reasons, poor nations remain poor and the hungry remain hungry.

The Global Agribusiness System

Let's look at the problem of hunger in terms of today's political and economic institutions, focusing not on the numbers of people on the land, but on the way in which the growing of food has become part of the global agribusiness system. There are many cultures around the world where subsistence farming is still carried out, and there are hundreds of millions of small farmers who, though they may sell some crops, still use the land to feed themselves. But the farms that feed the world are almost all commercialized operations, and most farmers sell their crops in the marketplace in return for cash to pay for their needs, including foods they don't grow, rent, taxes, interest on loans, and the costly technological inputs of modern, high-output farming. Even most of the small subsistence farmers are part of this cash economy in some way, if not so much through the modern technology they use, then through the income they must earn to cope with rent and debt. In a cash economy, the distribution of food is determined not by demand, in the sense of who needs food, but by "effective" demand, that is, by who can pay for it. Whether a country has a high or a low population density, whether it has a great deal or hardly any arable land, whether it produces large quantities or almost no quantities of food within its borders, the one thread that runs consistently through almost every case is the association of hunger and the absence of an adequate source of income. Unemployment and underemployment are the real scourge of the hungry nations, and since the underdeveloped countries, where most hunger can be found, are still largely agrarian societies, this means that poverty and hunger are concentrated among the farmers.

We have already discussed some of the reasons for this. Around the world, modern farmers are caught in a terrible cost-price squeeze. Tractors, harvester-combines, irrigation pumps, and even simpler agricultural machinery, as well as fertilizers, pesticides, and seeds, have a relatively high fixed cost because of the labor required to manipulate industrial materials and produce these inputs. But that same technology makes it easier and cheaper to grow abundant harvests, and the surplus food that is produced drives down the prices farmers receive for their crops on world markets, sometimes below their production costs. Over time, this drives millions of the smaller farmers into debt and bankruptcy. Often, the decision to give up is not theirs to make. Tenant farmers and landless farmworkers are driven from the land by wealthy landowners and corporations who feel the same cost-price squeeze and attempt to reduce their labor costs through more mechanization or who clear the land of small cultivators to replant it with more profitable crops. Sometimes it is simply less trouble to leave large areas of land fallow, unplanted, even though thousands of people for whom profit is not the goal could live productively off this land. In *Roots of Rebellion*, Tom Barry reports that in Guatemala 25 percent of the most fertile land is left idle by large landowners. He also notes that "The swelling workforce means that estate owners rarely have to increase wages to find farmworkers."[2]

The number of people who farm has been in decline everywhere in the world throughout modern history. In the Western nations, an expanding industrial base has been able to absorb and to re-employ people thrown off the land, but in the Third World such an industrial modernization simply doesn't take place. Displaced agriculturalists in the underdeveloped nations simply become the landless rural poor, perhaps working as tenants on the larger and more successful commercial farms, perhaps not working at all, or perhaps leaving rural areas to crowd into the new slums and shantytowns surrounding the major cities of these countries. It is difficult for Americans to grasp this process, because our country has ample land and relatively few farmers. But in most underdeveloped countries there is relatively little arable land worked by many farmers on small plots, and mechanization and agricultural technology reduce the labor required to farm and put people out of work.

Industrialization to re-employ these people fails in the Third World for historical and political reasons. During the eighteenth and nineteenth centuries, the Western powers chose conquest and economic control of Africa, Asia, and Latin America, rather than a policy of simple free trade, to ensure their food security. In the process, the economies of the conquered countries during the age of imperialism were re-oriented to produce agricultural products desired by the Europeans. Where there had existed complex, self-sufficient economies, there soon arose streamlined agricultural systems, utilizing plantation-style monoculture, producing large quantities of a few basic commodities for export—cereal grains, meat, coffee, cocoa, tea, cotton, rubber, sugar, and so on. Industrial technology was only introduced where it was useful in the extraction of other raw materials such as iron ore, tin, copper, and precious metals such as gold and silver. Nowhere did the European powers promote a comprehensive program of industrial modernization in Third World countries, because manufactures were the key to their economic dominance, and the last thing they wanted was new competitors. It was much more useful to have many underdeveloped countries competing to exchange the same basic farm staples and raw materials, because it made those products cheap.

Under the new global agribusiness system, direct political control of the underdeveloped nations has largely passed from the scene. But the nature of their agrarian economies and what they are able to produce has not changed. In a subtler way, economic control is maintained under current theories of free trade and comparative advantage, and the strategies Western aid experts suggest to promote economic development in the poorer nations. Theories of free trade date back to the time of the British economist Adam Smith, the great theorist of free markets. As industrial capitalism emerged in Great Britain, Smith was engaged in a great debate against the prevailing theory of mercantilism, which said that an economically powerful nation should erect trade barriers to keep out cheap imports that would compete with products manufactured at home. Smith argued that free trade would increase competition, lower the prices consumers paid for goods, and improve economic efficiency by allocating production to those regions of the world where goods could be produced more cheaply. With his theory of comparative advantage, Smith demonstrated that even if you could not produce any goods more cheaply than other countries, it still paid to trade freely, because within your own country some goods could be produced more efficiently than others, and by focusing on those goods your own labor would be used to better purpose, and overall production and prosperity would increase.

Changes in Trade

Smith's arguments have triumphed among modern economists, and in recent years GATT, NAFTA, and the integration of the European Economic Community (EEC) have all been efforts to break down trade barriers and make free trade a global reality. But because the world is now divided into advanced regions selling expensive, high-technology products and less advanced regions selling cheap raw materials and farm products, free-trade policies have transferred the cost-price squeeze from individual farmers to entire nations. In the last twenty years, instead of undergoing modernization, underdeveloped nations have been slowly transferring their wealth back to the industrialized nations, incurring greater and greater national debt in the process. The theory of comparative advantage, as applied to the underdeveloped nations, asserts that their climates and lands are best suited to the growing of tropical crops—coffee, bananas, cotton, cocoa—the crops desired by the developed nations, though in fact these countries can grow a wide variety of foods. The majority of underdeveloped nations depend for as much as 90 percent of their export earnings on only one or two of these export crops, overproducing them and glutting world markets, driving prices down.

When the production of cash crops in a glutted world market proves to be unprofitable, an underdeveloped nation experiences an unfavorable balance of trade. An unfavorable balance of trade occurs when one country exports to another country fewer goods, or goods of less value, than it receives from the other country. The difference in value must be made up by paying the other country with cash reserves, just as the medieval princes had to do to obtain their spices from Arab and Venetian merchants. When those cash reserves are depleted, the disadvantaged country must either stop purchasing foreign goods or borrow money and go into debt to maintain its trade. Third World nations experiencing debt problems in the 1960s and 1970s turned to foreign commercial banks and foreign governments for loans. But unable to solve their balance-of-trade problems, their debts continued to build up until private banks and individual foreign governments could no longer extend credit. The only remaining alternative for underdeveloped nations was to turn to international development banks for loans. Two of the most active such international banks are the World Bank and the International Monetary Fund (IMF), founded in the 1940s at the end of World War II to promote free trade and economic development.

Loans and Debt

The World Bank and the IMF regard themselves as lenders of last resort, providers of low-interest loans when debt-ridden governments can no longer obtain credit from commercial banks or other governments. But these lenders are controlled and financed by the industrialized nations, and completely dedicated to the theory of free markets. Opening up underdeveloped nations for more trade and increasing the size of Third World markets for Western products is an integral part of their thinking in making loans. Their loans, consequently, come with conditions. The bankers and their development experts will sit down with representatives of the government requesting the loan and work out what has been called a structural readjustment program, an economic strategy the debtor nation must follow to continue receiving credit. Unfortunately, many of these readjustment programs are quite harsh on indebted economies, and the economic strategies have often backfired and led to even more widespread poverty and hunger.

Such readjustment programs are likely to include demands for the removal of tariffs and trade barriers on imported manufactures and luxury goods, as well as elimination of any restrictions on the free flow of Western investment capital into or out of the country. In underdeveloped countries, the effect of freely imported Western goods is often the destruction of local industries and handicraft operations, throwing more people out of work, as well as the siphoning of limited cash reserves back to the industrialized countries. Inflowing Western capital, if it is invested in agriculture at all, is usually invested in large-scale commercial farming operations that compete with and threaten smaller farms. Adjustment programs also usually require privatization policies, where Third World governments are encouraged to sell off to private companies supposedly inefficient public utilities and state-owned industries, and to eliminate state subsidies and price controls. The immediate effect of such policies is felt most strongly by the urban poor, who must deal with increases in the rates charged for water, electricity, public transport, and even bread. The elimination of state subsidies to local industries puts them at a competitive disadvantage with the multinational firms in their own local markets and leads to their demise or takeover by foreign companies. Third World governments are asked to make their operations smaller and to reduce national expenditures, and this usually means cuts to local health, education, and welfare programs. Privatization and cuts in government spending also mean unemployment and lower wages for civil service workers. Another demand is currency devaluation, so that a dollar or a yen or a franc is worth more of the local currency. The theory behind this is that it will make exports from the debtor nations cheaper in world markets, more attractive to purchasers, and therefore earn back more foreign exchange. But in world markets glutted with unsold grain already being offered at low prices, currency devaluation does not often give the competitive edge it should, and within the debtor nation it makes foreign imports more expensive, at a time when other parts of the adjustment program are encouraging more dependence on imports. More cash flows out of the debtor nation, until trade actually declines because people can no longer afford to buy so many foreign imports with their deflated currency.

The strategy recommended by the Third World's creditors is a strategy of belt-tightening and self-destructive trade policies. Reduce expenditures and keep producing more goods for export, even if those goods become worth less and less in international markets, and their cheap prices benefit the developed nations buying them. In a cycle of cash flow that would seem almost conspiratorial, the money loaned to the underdeveloped nations goes back to the transnational corporations who control their imports, who provide the new agricultural technology, who own the new export-oriented farms, and who manage the construction of development projects.

All these and other measures demanded by the World Bank and the IMF have had the effect of opening up vulnerable, underdeveloped economies to the full force of Western commerce and industry, which may bring some economic growth in terms of increasing gross national product (GNP), but which carries out the same violent transformation of the underdeveloped economy that was experienced over a longer period during the development of capitalism in Europe. Millions of rural poor are being thrown off the land, without, however, a corresponding industrial take-off to reabsorb them, and they have formed a vast army of the hungry. The loan and development policies of the industrialized nations have failed to take account of the fact that in the Third World poverty is a rural phenomenon, that mechanizing and commercializing agriculture for export production reduces rural employment, so that even if these export crops could be sold at a decent price, fewer people would receive the benefits.

The damage done to underdeveloped economies only makes it more difficult to repay development loans, and during the 1980s many countries, especially those of South and Central America, experienced a debt crisis requiring massive new loans and slower rates of repayment to the Western banks. Today, the poorer nations of the world have accumulated more than $1 trillion in debt. The nations of Latin America and the Caribbean alone owe more than $400 billion. A significant portion of the new loans must be used to pay off the old debt in a never-ending cycle that prevents the use of this money for modernization and development. Since 1982, underdeveloped nations have actually been paying back to foreign banks about $30 billion more than they receive in new credit.

There are other forces at work that prevent these billions of dollars in development funds from helping to create the kind of modern economies that can build local enterprises, put their people to work, and achieve the levels of prosperity enjoyed by the industrialized nations. We have already discussed the obstacles to development imposed by free trade policies and the monopoly Western nations have on high technology. But within the underdeveloped nations themselves, political forces often work against development. Many Third World countries are ruled by authoritarian governments and military juntas. Even where this is not the case, these countries are likely to be ruled from one major city where a small urban elite—composed of bureaucrats and civil servants, traditional wealthy families and landowners, businesspeople, and the better-off workers—forms a ruling party and controls the nation's future. These are the very groups whose welfare is so closely tied to free-trade policies and the inflow of Western luxury goods. Though they live in nations where the majority of the people live in the countryside, and where poverty and hunger are concentrated among the rural poor, these elites tend to see "development" in terms of urban modernization, improvements in the middle-class lifestyle of city dwellers through high technology imported from the richer nations, and whatever policies or projects increase their prosperity and cement their hold on power. They want, in essence, to mimic the lifestyle they see in Western magazines and films.

Under such a power structure, development funds are often used for prestige projects, such as a modern airport, hospital, highway system, or new government buildings. These projects give the urban elite a sense of living in a modern society, but they can do very little for the rural poor. Other projects, such as hydroelectric dams to provide electric power for the cities and irrigation water for the larger commercial farms and plantations, rarely supply electricity to the rural poor and often flood the land where the poorest farmers live. There is rarely any meaningful effort to promote the kind of rural development that will provide income security for the farmers. A common practice of authoritarian governments is to keep the price of staple foods low in urban marketplaces. This tends to suppress political discontent in the cities but prevents farmers from earning an adequate income. Whatever rural aid is given is usually in the form of agricultural technology that makes farming more expensive and gives the richer farmers more of an edge over the poorer farmers. The richer farmers are usually producing cash crops for export, and as they prosper and absorb more of the poorer farmers' land, less and less land is given over to the production of foods for local consumption, creating more hunger. And, of course, since hunger, poverty, and class divisions create political instability, a good portion of development money is used by many Third World governments to build up a strong military that can suppress movements for change. During the 1980s, more than 80 percent of all U.S. aid to foreign countries was in the form of military aid.

This raises the more general question of the purpose of foreign aid.

Though they frequently talked about bringing civilization to the uncivilized, the nations of eighteenth- and nineteenth-century Europe clearly had their own interests in mind when they undertook to colonize Africa, Asia, and Latin America. Today's foreign aid programs, unfortunately, often suffer from a similar gap between rhetoric and reality. Many people in the industrialized nations believe that their aid to developing countries is motivated by compassionate benevolence, and many others resent the giving away of so much money to distant and ungrateful foreigners. Both views are based on false impressions.

Food Aid

First of all, far less money is "given away" than people realize. Foreign aid represents no more than one-fifth of 1 percent of the gross national product (GNP) of the United States. More than half of the food aid provided by the United States is in the form of loans to foreign governments to purchase U.S. grain. That money is returned to American farmers and merchants, increasing their income, helping to reduce agricultural surpluses, and supporting higher farm prices. And the money must be paid back at some point. Only about 10 percent of U.S. food aid is in the form of free emergency food relief. Dumping large quantities of food into an underdeveloped nation may help to stave off immediate starvation, if the government resells that food at a price that poor people can pay, but it also drives down the price of food in local markets to the point that small farming operations become even more unprofitable, and it may drive many poor farmers off the land, creating more poverty and hunger, undermining the local farm economy and increasing dependence on imported food supplies. This benefits corporations in the industrialized countries who are looking to open up larger markets for their food products in the poorer countries, damaging efforts to develop local industries and increasing unemployment. In the late 1960s, for

Food aid to underdeveloped nations provides immediate relief but does not solve more long-term problems within those countries.

example, economic assistance provided by the United States to South Korea was given with the stipulation that it be used to promote the livestock and poultry industries, and that restrictions on agricultural imports be removed. This paved the way for Cargill, Inc., and Ralston Purina to establish poultry plants in South Korea supported by their own grain sales. By the early 1970s, South Korea had become dependent on American imports of feed grain. Similar agreements increased the importation of American wheat, literally changing the eating habits of South Koreans as their government was able to export more of the nation's rice crop.

The food aid may even be used by an undemocratic government to postpone genuine land reform or other programs designed to distribute resources more equitably. The military government of Bangladesh receives about $1.5 million in U.S. food aid every year and has consistently refused to carry out is own land reform programs, programs that might increase food production and eliminate the need for U.S. aid. More than 90 percent of this aid is used to provide low-cost food to the urban middle class in Dacca, though more than 85 percent of the nation's people live in the countryside and that is where poverty is concentrated. In 1976, the United States embassy in Dacca informed the State Department that "The incentive for Bangladesh government leaders to devote attention, resources, and talent to the problem of increasing domestic food-grain production is reduced by the security provided by U.S. and other donors' food assistance."[3]

Food aid may also be used as a political weapon. A review of where our food aid has gone reveals that it often does not go to the most needy countries but to our staunchest allies and nations that support our foreign-policy objectives. According to the U.S. Agency for International Development, during the early 1980s the greatest portion of foreign economic assistance went to countries such as Israel and Egypt, where the United States wishes to maintain a strong political presence because of Middle Eastern oil, and to dictatorships such as El Salvador, Bangladesh, and the Philippines. The poorest countries of Africa received less than 5 percent of U.S. economic assistance during the same period. During the early 1970s, most U.S. aid was directed to the countries of Southeast Asia to bolster their support for the American military effort in Vietnam. Food aid is used as an instrument of foreign policy, and it is rarely given out of pure benevolence. And all too often, the governments of the United States and other industrialized countries view their national interests as being best promoted by strong alliances with Third World dictatorships that have little desire to bring about economic reform. This, too, is part of the legacy of colonialism—the belief that those nations who desire economic independence, political reform, and food self-sufficiency are our enemies.

Even food aid from nonprofit, voluntary organizations can have devastating consequences for underdeveloped nations. The legions of NGOs (non-government organizations) engaged in food relief and transfer of Western agricultural technology to the poor nations too often tend to see the solutions to the world's food problems in terms of increasing food production rather than democratizing food distribution, and to some critics they have become part of the problem. In 1993, in a speech before Cornell University graduate students preparing for aid work in underdeveloped countries, Michael Maren spoke of his work as an aid worker in Somalia in 1981. "It was clear to many of us, even then, that the program was working to prop up a corrupt dictator and turn nomads into relief junkies. . . . Somalia had actually produced a surplus of food that year, yet PVOs [private voluntary organizations] continue to distribute free food and collect U.S. government money for administering the delivery. Inevitably, indigenous food-distribution networks withered and died. The country's economy adapted to foreign aid—not to production."[4]

Promoting Famine

Inequities in political and economic power between nations can be so oppressive that when a natural disaster comes along, such as a flood or a drought or a crop-destroying pest, chronic poverty and malnutrition become acute starvation. One of the most painful illustrations comes not from Africa or Asia, but from northern Europe, the *An Gorta Mor*, the great Irish potato famine of 1845 to 1849. In the twelfth century, Pope Adrian gave Ireland to King Henry II of England, little suspecting that later English monarchs would forsake Catholicism. In the centuries that fol-

In the 1800s, the Irish became dependent upon potatoes, so when the crop failed, they began to starve.

lowed, under the Tudor kings and queens, Oliver Cromwell, and William III, a series of land confiscations took place that turned Ireland into a nation of landless peasants working the farms of absentee English landlords. The Irish sank into poverty, and their lives were so harsh that their English masters regarded them as uncivilized savages. It is no exaggeration to say that the English literally pushed the Irish into the ground. Many of the poorest tenant farmers lived in *scalpeens*, which were holes in the earth covered with rags and pieces of old furniture.

The Irish grew a variety of crops, including wheat, oats, rye, and barley, but these were cash crops grown for export back to England so that the Irish tenant farmers could earn money to pay their rent, the English landlords could realize an income from their property, and the English working class could be fed. For their own nourishment, the Irish had become completely dependent on one root crop brought through Europe from South America—the potato. In the particularly damp weather of 1845, the Irish potato crop was attacked by a fungus scientists call *Phytophtera infestans*, known more commonly as "the late blight." By 1846 and 1847, the potato crop had failed completely, and the Irish began to starve. The tenant farmers faced an impossible choice—continue to sell their other crops to pay their rents while starving to death or eat their cash crops instead of selling them, default on their rents, suffer eviction from their land, and without any means of livelihood, again, starve to death. Evictions did not trouble the English landlords, for they had a vision of clearing the land of all of its small-scale farms and reorganizing them into larger, more profitable farms to grow wheat and pasture cattle. Charles Wood, Britain's chancellor of the exchequer, wrote to a landlord, "I am not at all appalled by your tenantry going. This seems to me a necessary part of the process. . . . We must not complain of what we really want to obtain."

The British Parliament passed Poor Laws to establish workhouses for the dispossessed and imported corn from the United States to feed the Irish. But these charitable measures were inadequate, because the British politicians, under the influence of laissez-faire economic theories, did not want to give away so much food that market prices would collapse and hurt British merchants. The Irish socialist James Connolly wrote of these politicians, "They stood for the rights of property and free competition and philosophically accepted their consequences for Ireland." In many cases, the handling of the famine was motivated less by economic principle than by self-interest. The British foreign secretary, Lord Palmerston, was one of the biggest absentee landlords, and obtained half of his income from his Irish estates. Altogether, between 1846 and 1853, the English spent less than £10 million ($16 million) on famine relief in Ireland. By comparison, between 1853 and 1856, they spent almost £70 million ($112 million) to fight the Crimean War and protect their "passage to India."

The absentee landlords were taxed to pay for this food relief, and believing themselves relieved of moral responsibility for the famine, they felt justified in continuing their evictions at an even faster pace. The hunger grew worse. Commenting on the situation of the Irish peasantry in December 1849, the *Illustrated London News* reported that "The ruin is great and complete. It came in the guise of charity . . . and it has struck them to the heart. They are prostrate and helpless. The once frolicsome people—even the saucy beggars—have disappeared, and given place to wan and haggard objects, who are so resigned to their doom, that they no longer expect relief. One beholds only shrunken frames scarcely covered with flesh—crawling skeletons, who appear to have risen from their graves." Between 1845 and 1854, more than a million Irish people starved to death, and another 1.6 million emigrated to America. Writing during the Christmas season of 1848, a reporter for the *Tipperary Vindicator* commented, "The work of undermining the population is going on stealthily, but steadily. . . . Whole districts are cleared. . . . There are vast tracts of the most fertile land in the world in this noble country now thrown out of tillage. . . . The howl of misery has succeeded the merry carol which used to usher in the season. . . ." And throughout this period, Ireland never stopped exporting food.

From 1968 to 1974, half a million people and 5 million cattle died during the drought in sub-Saharan Africa.

In more recent times, there have been equally terrible famines precipitated by natural disasters, but in almost every case there is an underlying cause related to the control or ownership of land and economic resources. From 1968 to 1974, in the Sahelian countries of sub-Saharan Africa—Senegal, Mauritania, Mali, Niger, Chad, and the Central African Republic—a prolonged drought killed half a million people and 5 million cattle. In addition to being too dry, the experts said, the land had been overgrazed, implying that the herders of cattle, goats, and sheep who lived in the region had somehow done themselves in. But it was the Western development experts who had encouraged the livestock farmers to expand their herds in an effort to provide more beef for export to Europe. They provided the herders with Western technology to do so—antibiotics to make the cattle healthier and well-digging equipment to provide more water. The Sahelian pastoralists had no choice but to cooperate, because Europe was their only market. The trouble was that while new wells can draw more water, they cannot create pastureland, and the larger herds of hungry cattle ate the grass down to its roots, denuding the land of all vegetation and turning it into desert. The cattle died, and the herders crowded into the cities and refugee centers for food aid. Looking at all these livestock farmers trying to live on less and less pastureland, Western experts declared that the Sahel was overpopulated. In the western countries of the Sahel, the French had encouraged farmers to plant more and more land with peanuts and cotton to satisfy the European demand for peanut oil and cheap textiles. But peanuts withdraw nutrients from the soil at alarming rates. "Just two successive years of peanuts," report Francis Moore Lappé and Joseph Collins, "can rob the soil of Senegal of almost a third of its organic matter." And the U.S. cotton planters of the antebellum South had to put new land under cultivation every seven years because of the destructive effects of cotton on the soil. The drought only precipitated a crisis that had been in the making for many years, as a result of international trading patterns and the dependence of Sahelian farmers on the whims of foreign consumers.

A famine in Bengal in 1943 killed more than 2 million people, but there was no shortage of food in the country. An economic boom had simply raised the price of rice to the point where the poor could not afford it. In 1974, floods in Bangladesh destroyed most of the harvest, but the government refused to appropriate large stores of available rice and distribute them. It was too dependent on the foreign exchange it could obtain by selling its food stocks abroad. Merchants exported the rice to India, while tens of thousands starved. *National Geographic* magazine reported that "Despite loss of foodstuffs, however, there is an estimated four million tons of rice in Bangladesh during the famine—enough to feed the entire nation for a third of the year." One could go on and on, and we have not even mentioned the famines caused by other human activities, such as war and revolution. From 1967 to 1969, famine induced by civil war killed 1.5 million people in Biafra. In this case, the Nigerian government literally used food as a weapon, cutting off supplies to its rebellious province in order to starve the separatist army. From 1975 to 1979, motivated by an insane ideology of destroying the urban middle class and all educated professionals and building an egalitarian society of peasants, the Khmer Rouge of Cambodia starved to death at least a million people. Much less well known is the famine that occurred in China in the early 1960s, when Mao Zedong reorganized agriculture into large-scale communes, expecting farm output to increase as a result. Because of the top-down, bureaucratic structure of the government, fearful local officials in rural areas simply lied to their superiors and reported vastly increased harvests. The lies worked well enough until the central government collected its share of the grain, which was apportioned on the basis of inflated figures, leaving inadequate supplies of food for the people in the countryside. The causes of famine are complex, but they have more to do with human institutions and policies than with available food supplies.

Mexico

Mexico presents an interesting example of how the commercialization of agriculture, free trade, and structural readjustment programs can damage the food self-sufficiency of a nation. Since the 1950s, Green Revolution technology in Mexico had consolidated land in the hands of the wealthier farmers, and by the 1970s many of the wealthier farmers were switching from corn to sorghum. Sorghum was in demand as livestock feed for a growing number of cattle ranchers, who had driven poor *campesinos* off their subsistence farms to produce beef for export. Domestic corn production

Much of Mexico is wealthy, yet nearly 50 percent still live in poverty.

declined, and today Mexico imports about 25 percent of its corn and is no longer self-sufficient in the production of this staple food. Increading rural poverty is the by-product of a small number of feed-growers and cattle ranchers being able to bring in more export income. Development funds have gone in and out of the country rapidly as urban Mexicans purchase more imported foods and manufactures and transnational corporations are paid to "improve" agriculture, and Mexico's foreign debt increased.

Since its debt crisis of 1982 and the rescheduling of its loan repayments, Mexico has dutifully carried out the structural readjustment program demanded by the International Monetary Fund. One of the requirements was a reduction in public spending. Mexico cut its health budget in half, and between 1980 and 1992 the number of infant deaths caused by nutritional

The tortilla, Mexico's staple food, is an unleavened bread made from corn.

deficiencies tripled. Credit has been given mainly to those farmers with the potential to export their crops, hurting the smaller producers of corn and beans, the principal staple foods. A wave of privatization has encouraged foreign corporations to purchase ownership of banks and businesses throughout the country. In the wake of NAFTA in 1994, more than 250,000 Mexicans lost their jobs as cheap foreign imports undermined domestic industries. A financial crisis ensued, forcing devaluation of the currency and requiring $51 billion in United States loans to prevent economic collapse. Urban unemployment has reached 15 percent of the workforce. Nearly 50 percent of the entire population live in conditions of poverty, and disparities in wealth between the rich and the poor are increasing. The wealthiest Mexican, Carlos Slim, who owns the Mexican telephone utility, has a net worth of $6.6 billion, more than the combined income of the poorest 20 percent of the population—17 million people who subsist on a little more than $300 a year.

The staple food of millions of poor Mexicans is the tortilla, an unleavened bread made from corn. The kernels of corn are boiled in water and lime, ground into a pliable dough, pressed into flat cakes, and cooked. Traditionally, tortillas were prepared by thousands of small shops all over the country. They received their corn from Conasupo, the government commodities distribution agency that controlled the entire corn harvest. Conasupo subsidized corn production by paying farmers a price far above the market value of their corn, and then selling it to the thousands of tortilla-makers at low prices. It was then able to set a ceiling on the price of cooked tortillas in the marketplace, ensuring that consumers would enjoy cheap tortillas, the tortilla shops could still make a profit, and farmers would receive an adequate income, all at a cost of about $1 billion dollars to the government and the Mexican taxpayer.

Under the terms of the structural readjustment program it had agreed to in order to obtain foreign credit, the corrupt administration of President Carlos Salinas de Gotari was under pressure to change this system. A close political ally of the Salinas family and a big contributor to the governing Institutional Revolutionary Party, businessman Roberto Gonzalez Barrera discovered a way to replace fresh corn dough with a processed corn flour by cooking the dough in a kind of blast furnace. With loans from the Salinas family and the government, he created the corporate giant Grupo Industrial Maseca and began to build factories to produce this corn flour. He sold special machines to the better-off tortilla shops so that they could use his processed corn flour instead of taking the time to prepare the fresh dough. In 1990, the Salinas government decided to freeze the amount of corn that was sold to the traditional tortilla-makers and marketed its corn to the Maseca corporation instead, insisting that all growth in the tortilla industry be based on processed corn flour. If a tortilla shop refused the new machine and the processed flour, the government made sure that it received only the worst corn. As a result, Gonzalez, who is known in Mexico as the "King of Tortillas," cornered more than 90 percent of the domestic corn flour market and built up a personal fortune of more than $1 billion, while hundreds of small tortilla shops went out of business. The Maseca corporation has now expanded into other areas of Latin America and even into the United States under the corporate name of Mission Foods. Though the Salinas family lost control of the government in 1994, Gonzalez is still a powerful figure courted by the politicians, and under the new privatization program he has purchased two of the largest national banks. Thousands of small tortilla shopkeepers are now out of work, adding to urban poverty, and the remaining shops are dependent on equipment supplied by one corporation. Mexicans are compelled to buy a new processed food that many feel is inferior in taste. The system of government-subsidized corn distribution now enriches one large monopoly. Thanks to economic "liberalization" and NAFTA, corn and beans are the only remaining foodstuffs under government price controls, and if these are eliminated, tortilla prices will rise under the market dominance of the Maseca corporation, and fewer poor consumers will be able to afford them.

The stranglehold of debt, poverty, rural and urban unemployment, land concentration, and export-oriented agriculture controlled by the wealthiest farmers and the transnational corporations have all contributed to a national economic crisis that increases hunger, malnutrition, illness, and political instability, and the rebellion of the Zapatistas in the state of Chiapas is only the most recent manifestation of the desperation of poor farmers. This situation has been repeated innumerable times throughout Central and South America, Africa, and Asia, with twists and turns that would be fascinating if the results were not so tragic. We have come a long way from the tyrants of the ancient city-states and the masses who labored in the mud of the river valleys, ever fearful that the sun-god or the rain-god would desert them and bring down famine upon them. But the hungry are still with us, and democratic control over the production and distribution of food resources still eludes us. The next and last chapter will try to suggest some solutions to the crisis.

Chapter Six
The Future of Food

As we have seen, the proposition that too many people are trying to subsist on too little food is an insupportable argument in the world today. Nevertheless, if present trends continue, the population of the world is likely to increase to perhaps 8 million or 10 billion people sometime in the twenty-first century. Then human pressure on the food supply will be a very real issue. If our future goal is to live in a world where there is no hunger, we will have to deal with several interrelated questions. Can rates of population growth be reduced, or will they fall naturally if increased global prosperity provides greater family security? And if not, can we find ways to produce more food? And if we can, will we be able to distribute this food more equitably? What theory of modernization will work for the underdeveloped countries—one that opposes the integration of the global economy and makes each nation self-sufficient in food production, or one that encourages world trade and a real program of industrialization so that the poorer nations can become rich enough to buy the food they can't grow?

Can we produce more food? One answer to that question is to

Harvesting quinoa in Bolivia. There is new interest in cultivating this grain as well as amaranth.

exploit new sources of food. It is somewhat startling to realize that, of the hundreds of edible food plants, only about twenty species have been chosen by human beings as staple foods. These species have been highly successful as food plants, of course, and people tend to be conservative in their eating habits anyway. But in recent years, farmers and scientists have been experimenting with new varieties of crops. Amaranth and quinoa are cereal grains that have been grown in the Americas since ancient times, but new hybrid varieties of the plants and improved techniques of processing them are generating increasing interest in their cultivation. Cassava, a root crop that was not widely grown outside the tropics before 1900, has now become a major staple food for 500 million people around the world. The sago palm has become an important food for the peoples of Melanesia, and mushrooms are becoming more important in the diets of people in central Africa.

Grains, Leaves, and Bacteria

Research into the traditional cereal grains has not been neglected. Scientists are working on new strains of wheat that will thrive in soils and climates previously thought to be unsuitable for agriculture. The Chinese are experimenting with a new hybrid variety of rice that is expected to increase yields by 75 percent and a new variety of sweet sorghum that can be used for livestock feed and for fermenting into alcohol for fuel. Plant geneticists are attempting to transfer to the rice plant the legume's ability to fix nitrogen in the soil, so that less fertilizer is required to grow the rice. Egypt has already begun exporting a hybrid fava bean, and scientists have developed a new hybrid pigeon pea that will vastly increase the food value of legumes. There are thousands of seeds, fruits, nuts, and pods in the plant world, especially in our tropical rain forests, that have yet to be studied.

We usually eat the seed heads of food plants and discard the rest or feed it to our animals. The conventional wisdom is that leaves and stems can provide us with some fiber, but little of real nutritional value. But the leaves of young plants contain quite a bit of protein. We would have to chew our way through an enormous amount of this roughage to obtain a significant amount of this protein, but if it could be extracted from the leaves beforehand, it might become an important source of food with a protein level

Rain forests produce a wide variety of seeds and pods that we still do not fully understand.

equal to that of soybeans or fish meal. The British scientist N. W. Pirie has designed a special machine that grinds leaves into a pulp and then presses out a protein-rich juice. The juice can be processed into a dark green cake with the consistency of cheese, or a powder-like condensed milk. Some experiments in the commercial production of leaf protein have been undertaken in different parts of the world. In India, the cake is flavored with a spicy curry, and in Africa it is used as a base for soups. In powder form, it can be added to many foods as a protein supplement, and the waste products from the extraction process can be used as livestock feed.

Microorganisms such as bacteria and yeasts are also being studied as potential food sources. Grown in indoor tanks where the "farmers" don't have to worry about the weather, these microbes can be fed an odd assortment of nutrients, such as petroleum by-products and old newspapers. One such organism, SCP, or single-cell protein, is being grown in large enough quantities to be fed to livestock. At oil refineries in France, Russia, and the United States, paraffin is extracted from crude oil and fed to yeasts, which are able to convert 1 ton (.9 mt) of paraffin into one-half ton (.4 mt) of pure protein. Scientists in Japan and Czechoslovakia are also experimenting with Chlorella, a single-celled, protein-rich algae, growing liquid cultures in tanks placed on top of greenhouses. If a way can be found to discard the algae's cell walls and extract the protein from inside the cell, it may become an important source of food.

Animals and Insects

Beyond the world of plants, other experiments are taking place. Many insects, for example, are known to contain high levels of vitamins and minerals. Bee larvae contain more vitamin D than can be found in fish oil. Raising bees for honey, of course, is a very old form of animal husbandry. Few people realize, incidentally, the importance of the honey bee in pollinating our food plants. Without them, large-scale commercial agriculture in many parts of the world would probably collapse. New species of mammals are also being looked at as food sources. We have domesticated only about a dozen species of animals so far, but there are many wild animals that graze on land unsuitable for farming or for our present varieties of livestock. The eland, or African antelope, whose ancestors were eaten by the hunter-gatherers, produces a tender steak that has less fat than that of beef cattle,

Meat from the eland, or African antelope, is lower in fat than that of beef cattle.

and it has proven easy to herd. It also consumes less water and is resistant to the tsetse fly that kills so many cattle in tropical Africa. The gnu, or wildebeest, is another large species of antelope that may someday be used as a source of beef. In Uganda, efforts to protect the hippopotamus from hunters led to a hippo population explosion, and experiments in commercial hippo ranching are now underway. The adult hippopotamus weighs more than 3,000 pounds (1,360 kg) and produces more than 1,000 pounds (454 kg) of meat that is as nutritious as beefsteak.

There is also much speculation about the food value of the Arctic muskox, which can provide both nutritious meat and milk. Once an endangered species, it has been successfully raised in Alaska, and it can survive in cold regions of the world where no other cattle can survive. People who live in rain forests hunt a variety of small mammals like the peccary, the capybara, and the agouti. Though the meat is rather tough, domestication and selective breeding might produce more palatable species. The dugong, a large marine mammal found in the western Pacific, grazes on seaweed and algae and is hunted by the indigenous people of the region from dugout canoes. And though environmentalists may cringe, the manatee of tropical rivers, weighing between 500 and 2,000 pounds (227 and 907 kg), is an important source of meat for native hunters and may one day be raised in sea farms just as cattle are raised on land. Fish meal, now fed to livestock, has not been widely accepted as a direct source of food because of its peculiar taste and odor, but the Bureau of Commercial Fisheries in Beltsville, Maryland, has developed a fish meal known as fish protein concentrate (FPC) that is tasteless and odorless and may someday be added to other foods.

Research Centers

Today, there is a mind-boggling number of international research centers attempting to improve the food value of our traditional crops and livestock, and since the 1960s they have turned more of their attention to the food problems of the underdeveloped countries. We have already mentioned the International Rice Research Institute (IRRI) and the work of the Ford and Rockefeller Foundations. There is also the International Center of Tropical Agriculture (CIAT) in Cali, Colombia, working on new varieties of rice, beans, and cassava, and the International Crops Research Institute for the Semi-Arid Tropics (ICRISAT) in Andhra Pradesh, India, conducting research on millet, sorghum, chickpeas, and groundnuts. There is the

International Center for Improvement of Wheat and Maize (CIMMYT) in Lisboa, Mexico; the International Potato Center (CIP) in Lima, Peru; the West African Rice Development Association in Bouaké (WARDA), the Ivory Coast; the International Center for Living Aquatic Resources Management (ICLARM) in Manila, the Philippines; the International Plant Genetic Resources Institute (IPGRI) in Rome, Italy; the International Livestock Research Institute (ILRI) in Nairobi, Kenya; the International Institute of Tropical Agriculture (IITA) in Ibadan, Nigeria; the International Service for National Agricultural Research (ISNAR) in the Hague, the Netherlands; and the International Food Policy Research Institute (IFPRI) in Washington, D.C.

There are also more than twenty major plant gene banks located around the world, storing seeds and attempting through genetic engineering and molecular biology to create new ones. Privately owned commercial seed companies are also active in developing new plant varieties, but their work is controversial. The laws of many countries allow private firms to hold patents on the seeds they develop and to profit from their distribution. This makes the seeds expensive for underdeveloped nations and restricts their access to all this wonderful new biotechnology. In the United States, private control over new seed varieties was ensured by the Plant Variety Protection Act of 1970. Many seed companies are also owned by large, multinational petrochemical and pharmaceutical firms, such as Monsanto, Upjohn, Olin, Celanese, Ciba-Geigy, Royal Dutch Shell, and Occidental Petroleum, who have a natural reluctance to develop plants that require less fertilizer and pesticide, a tremendous expense for small farmers. In 1981, Thomas Urban of the Pioneer Hi-Bred Corn Company discussed the efforts of chemical companies to get into the hybrid seed business and admitted to a reporter for *The New York Times* that "The assumption behind the trend is that the new owners can improve the plant's resistance to the herbicides and pesticides that the parent company sells."[1] When the concept of a patent law was first conceived by Thomas Jefferson in 1790, it was to protect authors and inventors and allow them to profit from the labor of their work. But in the words of Jack Doyle, in his book *Altered Harvest*, "Among business interests, the patent is more a statement of territory than it is necessarily a measure of innovation."

Land Use

Where, however, will we grow all these new food plants, and where will we graze all these new animals? Only 11 percent of Earth's land surface is well suited for agriculture. The rest is either too dry, too wet, too shallow, permanently frozen, or chemically imbalanced for agriculture. There is some land that might be easily converted to farming or grazing land—indeed, some of it has already been converted—but few of us would support the destruction of the world's remaining forests. A portion of the land that is too dry or too wet might be put under cultivation through drainage or irrigation, but there are other problems with this strategy that we will get to in a moment. We must accept that there are limits to the amount of land available for farming and ranching activities, and, what is more discouraging, we are degrading the soil on that land at alarming rates, decreasing its capacity to produce abundant harvests. According to the Food and Agriculture Organization of the United Nations, soil erosion affects to some degree almost 5 billion acres (2 billion ha), or about 60 percent, of the best agricultural land. Every year, the world loses about 25 billion tons (22.7 billion mt) of topsoil; the United States alone loses about 3 billion tons (2.7 billion mt) a year, and each year the Huang Ho in China washes about 1.6 billion tons of (1.4 billion mt) topsoil into the ocean. Depending on the region and climate, it can take anywhere from 50 to 1,000 years for nature to rebuild as little as 1 inch (2.5 cm) of topsoil. According to the Global Tomorrow Coalition, "In many regions, rates of soil loss exceed rates of soil formation by at least tenfold."[2]

Most of this erosion is caused by the action of wind and water carrying the soil away, but this is not simply a natural phenomenon. The soil is carried away when there is insufficient vegetation to hold it in place. The destruction of vegetation is usually caused by human activities—clearing of forests, overgrazing of cattle, plowing too deeply, planting on steep slopes, failing to rotate crops, or working marginal lands beyond their capacity. These activities are not unrelated to the economic forces at work in the world and the global transition to large-scale, commercial agriculture. In the industrialized countries, mechanized farming techniques work the land very hard, and in addition to the causes just cited, continuous irrigation destroys the soil by raising its salt content, and the application of chemical fertilizers and pesticides sometimes poisons it. Salinization from excess irrigation has affected almost half of our cultivated land to some degree. In the underdeveloped countries, the expansion of larger farms and commercial operations producing cash crops for export drives poorer farmers and livestock ranchers onto marginal lands, which are the first to give out when farmed intensively. Soil erosion can be stopped through a variety of measures—building windbreaks and dams, terracing steeply sloping land, planting trees and soil-retaining crops such as alfalfa, rotating crops, shallow plowing and contour plowing—but until there are genuine changes in the forces driving the global agribusiness system, until there is real reform in undemocratic systems of land tenure and ownership, and until there is an authentic attack on the causes of rural poverty, it is unlikely that land degradation can be stopped.

Water Management

Efforts to put new lands under cultivation face serious obstacles. These lands will have poorer soils and will require greater agricultural inputs. One of the most important of these is water for irrigation. More than 97 percent of the world's water is sea water and is unusable for agriculture. Of

Earth's freshwater, almost 80 percent is permanently frozen in polar ice caps and glaciers and is also unusable. Almost another 20 percent of the freshwater supply is deep groundwater that is generally unavailable to us with our present technology. Less than 1 percent of the world's fresh water supply—in the form of surface ground water, rivers and lakes, and atmospheric water vapor—is available to us for all our needs, and agriculture is the largest user of that freshwater, consuming about 65 percent of the freshwater supply. Our present farming activities are rapidly using up that water. The availability of water is measured by the water table, the level below the surface of the ground where the earth still appears to be saturated with moisture, and the water table all around the globe is falling. The water table beneath the vast Ogallala Aquifer, which lies beneath eight of the most important agricultural states in the United States, is falling by about 3 feet (.9 m) a year. The water table beneath Beijing, the capital city of China, is falling by about 6 feet (1.83 m) every year. The level of soil moisture under Bangkok in Thailand has fallen by 75 feet (22.9 m) since 1950. Everywhere, our present agricultural activities, as well as industrial uses of water, and the needs of growing urban populations for water for drinking and sanitation, are using up our freshwater supplies. Already, one-third of the population of underdeveloped countries lacks adequate water for drinking and sanitation. Although only about 17 percent of the world's cultivated lands are artificially irrigated, those lands produce more than 30 percent of our food supply.

    Without radical conservation measures and wiser management of water resources, it is utopian to talk about putting more land under cultivation. Strategies and technologies to conserve water do exist. Wastewater can be purified and recycled. Urban populations can be taught to conserve water. With conventional irrigation systems, in some cases only about 40 percent of the water ever reaches the crops, but there are many new and more efficient systems—drip irrigation, low-pressure pivot sprays—that make more effective use of water. Large dams can be replaced by smaller ones located closer to farming areas, and canals can be lined and covered with materials that prevent seepage and evaporation. Out of necessity, many farmers around the world have put these new systems into practice. But here again, technology is subservient to economic forces. The worldwide growth of the large-scale, export-oriented, commercial farm, operating almost like a factory, producing food as a commodity, maximizing agricultural output at all costs, has tended to promote the wasteful use of agricultural resources, including water.

Fertilizers and Other Chemicals

The same can be said for other agricultural inputs. Putting new lands under cultivation will require more fertilizers, pesticides, fungicides, and other petrochemicals. Between 1950 and the mid-1980s, the world's use of fertilizer increased more than 900 percent, from 14 million tons (12.7 million mt) to more than 130 million tons (118 million mt). During the 1980s alone, fertilizer use increased from about 175 to 210 pounds (80 to 95 kg) per hectare (2.5 acres), but this is only average use. Most of the underdeveloped nations simply can't afford to use these amounts of fertilizer, but the Japanese use more than 880 pounds (400 kg) per hectare, the British about 770 pounds (350 kg) per hectare, the Chinese more than 620 pounds (280 kg), and the Egyptians more than 795 pounds (360 kg). There is a certain cruel irony in the Egyptian dependence on so much fertilizer. In ancient times, decaying vegetable matter in the Nile provided all the natural fertilizer the Egyptians needed. But with the completion of the Aswan High Dam on the upper Nile in 1970, built to provide the nation with cheap electricity, the flow of silt and nutrients to the lower river valley has been restricted, and much of the electric power produced by the dam must now be used to run the factories producing artificial fertilizer.

This tomato was destroyed by insects overnight. Some insects are resistant to pesticides and can destroy crops very quickly.

Rather than open up new lands for cultivation, the excessive use of fertilizer may degrade existing lands. The nitrogen and phosphates in commercial fertilizers can upset the natural chemical balance of soils and cause eutrophication of groundwater, which depletes the water of oxygen. Soil and water pollution is also a problem with pesticides. In the United States, pesticide use rose from 1 million pounds (453,600 kg) per year in the 1950s to more than 800 million pounds (363 million kg) per year in the late 1980s.

In India during the same period, pesticide use increased from 2,000 tons a year to more than 80,000 tons a year. It has been estimated that pesticide poisoning around the world kills about 40,000 people and is responsible for as many as 20,000 cases of cancer each year. And, of course, as insect pests adapt and develop resistance to these chemicals, the pesticides are less effective. Each year, well over 30 percent of the harvest in the United States is lost to insects. The Global Tomorrow Coalition reports that "This rate of crop loss to insects has nearly doubled since 1945, in spite of a tenfold increase in pesticide use."[3]

Again, there are many strategies available for reducing the amount of petrochemicals that we put into our farmland. "Fertigation" is a new technique whereby fertilizers can be applied more efficiently right at the roots of individual plants. Integrated Pest Management combines the intermixing of crops and new planting patterns with the genetic engineering of pest-resistant plants and the use of natural insect predators instead of chemical poisons. But some of these strategies are labor-intensive and are therefore not attractive to the operators of the large-scale, energy- and capital-intensive, commercial farms of the industrial agricultural system.

Farm Productivity

Whether we are talking about irrigation water or agrochemicals or, for that matter, farm machinery or genetically engineered seeds or finding new sources of food or cultivating more land, the conclusion we seem driven to is that the technological problems of agriculture are really economic problems. The type of large-scale, energy-intensive, commercial farming practiced in the industrialized nations and recommended for the underdeveloped nations may not be the appropriate model for the future. Such farms may increase agricultural output, since their primary purpose is to maximize cash income from the sale of crops, but are they really more efficient in terms of the tremendous costs of the industrial products we must apply to the land to increase our harvests? Large commercial farms produce a lot of food, but not necessarily the most food per unit of land. In *World Hunger: Twelve Myths*, Francis Moore Lappé and Joseph Collins report that "A recent study of 15 countries (primarily in Asia and Africa) found that per acre output on small farms can be four to five times higher than on large estates."[4] Large, plantation-style farms are often managed inefficiently by absentee owners, and much of their land may lie fallow and unplanted. Owners of smaller farms, out of necessity, must cultivate their land efficiently and show more concern for proper use of expensive agricultural inputs and soil conservation.

If large-scale commercial farming permanently degrades our soils, isn't the question of efficiency irrelevant in any case? Large-scale industrial agriculture may be *unsustainable* agriculture, not only in terms of land degradation, but in terms of its dependence on petroleum and petrochemicals. Oil does not exist in unlimited supplies, and as supplies dwindle, its cost will skyrocket. But this system of industrial farming does benefit certain interest groups with great economic power—the owners of the largest farms, the oil companies and chemical firms, the seed companies, the food-processing companies, the international grain traders, the banks and lending institutions, the small urban elite who control the economies of the underdeveloped nations, and the well-off consumers of the industrialized nations—and so the system persists. The commercial production of food as a commodity requires that food be turned into cash. If short-term profits are high enough, the system will be judged a success, regardless of its long-term unsustainablity.

Reform

How are we to deal with the problem of hunger in the world today, as well as the coming millions who must also be fed? We can't suggest detailed programs that would work for all countries, but from everything that has been said so far, it is possible to lay out a general approach, a series of ideas by which specific programs and policies might be judged. We will leave the problem of producing new foods and more food to the technocrats. It's a noble effort, but unless we can solve the problem of distributing food more equitably, the technocrats cannot eliminate hunger. Control of food resources is—and always has been—the issue.

We must, first of all, re-examine the role of industrial agriculture, large-scale commercial farming, and the export-oriented, commodity production of food—in terms of how efficiently it uses resources, whether it uses the land sustainably, how it tends to concentrate ownership of agricultural resources, and whether it effectively employs people in agrarian societies. With so much hunger, poverty, and unemployment concentrated in rural areas, it may be that smaller farms, more carefully managed and producing a greater diversity of basic food crops for local consumption, will both feed and employ greater numbers of people. The key to ending rural hunger is to keep as many people as possible employed as productive farmers and to increase their purchasing power. This is easy to say, but it implies radical changes in the world's agricultural systems. It requires real land reform: taking away the property of the wealthy and parceling it out to small landholders, breaking up the big estates and the holdings of the transnational corporations and ensuring through strong, enforceable laws that small farmers are granted inalienable rights to work their land. This kind of land reform has rarely been achieved anywhere in the world without courageous political leadership supported by mass, democratic movements, and so the struggle for political democracy in Third World countries is part of the solution. It also requires that citizens in the industrialized countries demand changes in the foreign policy of their governments—to withdraw support for dictatorial or corrupt regimes dominated by the interests of the rich.

The empowerment of small farmers also requires less expensive, alternative technologies for agriculture, techniques that don't raise the cost of farming and don't make it less labor-intensive, but do make it sustainable over the long term. We don't want to see a return to the era of backbreaking farm labor, but we must reduce the need for commercial fertilizers and pesticides through crop diversity, crop rotation, integrated pest management, and soil conservation. Mechanization only puts people out of work and is of more benefit to the Western manufacturers of farm machinery. Today, International Harvester obtains almost one-third of its sales from foreign purchasers; John Deere about 23 percent; and the Canadian farm machinery company Massey-Furguson obtains 70 percent of its sales from outside North America. This in spite of a study by the International Rice Research Institute that using a tractor does not produce any more rice than using a water buffalo. The purpose of agricultural technology should be to sustain the farmer, not to maximize the cash income from oil-fed crops, or to create greater divisions of wealth between large and small farms, or to provide markets for the products of high-tech industries. Small farmers will also need the development of marketing infrastructures that give them the same access to markets and storage and transportation facilities that the larger farmers and transnational corporations enjoy.

Eliminating Debt

Then there is the question of credit. Third World nations desperately need relief from, or cancellation of, their foreign debts that drain them of the financial resources they need for modernization. Many of these huge debts are already being rescheduled, since Third World nations are doing such a poor job of repaying their loans, but the bankers like to be quiet about these bad debts because of the financial panic it might cause if anyone stopped and realized that they will probably never be entirely repaid. A more overt and dramatic form of debt relief is required, and the citizens and businesses of the industrialized countries will have to absorb the loss, as Americans did during the recent scandal regarding bad loans on the part of savings and loan institutions. As painful as it may be, it is merely the recognition of reality. Debt swaps are an innovative technique first proposed by Thomas Lovejoy of the World Wildlife Fund in 1984 to save tropical rain forests. Conservation organizations with the cooperation of banks have purchased some of the debt of underdeveloped nations in exchange for promises to establish and maintain nature preserves in environmentally threatened regions. Perhaps a similar system of purchasing debt could be developed for nations that promise programs of land reform and economic development for small-scale staple food producers in rural areas.

Equally important is the need to provide small farmers in the underdeveloped nations with low-interest loans. Exorbitant interest rates charged by local moneylenders in agrarian societies are one of the prime causes of loss of farm ownership and concentration of land holdings. A pioneering effort was undertaken in Bangladesh in 1976 by Muhammad Yunus, founder of the Grameen (Village) Bank, who provided small farmers and landless peasants with low-interest loans averaging no more than $100, enough to purchase cows, seeds, and simple farming implements that ensured their survival without burdening them with excessive debt. By the early 1990s, the Grameen Bank had provided loans to 1.6 million farmers in 34,000 villages, usually small, five-member groups of women whose interdependent activities ensure that all will use the money appropriately. Each loan is so small that a default cannot possibly hurt the bank, though the rate of successful repayment is 98 percent. Studies indicate that Yunus' clients are prospering and maintain a better rate of loan repayment than those who depend on commercial lending programs. In addition to helping more than a million farmers to become self-supporting, Yunus, now a hero among his borrowers and progressive development experts, demonstrated that the poor have the intelligence and the will to succeed if they are given equal access to the resources they need. "We think of the poor differently," Yunus has said. "We think they are as capable and as enterprising as anybody else in the world. Circumstances have just pushed them to the bottom of the heap. They work harder than anybody else. They have more skills than they get a chance to use. With a supportive environment they can pull themselves out of the heap in no time."[5]

More than 90 percent of Grameen Bank loans are made to women, and this raises the issue of the special problems faced by women in Third World agriculture. When we talk about farming activities in agrarian societies, we are talking about work that is done predominantly by women. In these societies, women do between 30 percent and 50 percent of the plowing and planting, 50 percent of the work of raising livestock, 60 percent of the harvesting, and more than 80 percent of the work of processing and storing crops. They also have primary responsibility for feeding and raising children, as well as household and domestic work. Because of limited employment opportunities in poor agrarian societies, the men of these families are often forced into patterns of seasonal migration to find work far from home, and the farms are left in the care of the women and older children. A meaningful attack on global hunger and poverty requires special emphasis on the needs of women—in terms of equal rights before the law, the right to own land, education, family planning, and child welfare.

Another change of major proportions will have to be the reorientation of food aid and development loans. Direct food aid should only be given in dire emergencies, and even then only when it is clear that no stocks of food are being held in reserve by wealthy farmers, merchants, or the government receiving the aid. The purpose of food aid should be to alleviate famine, not to dispose of food surpluses in the industrialized nations so that farm prices can be supported, not to reward our political allies, not to maintain the employment of food aid workers, and not to take the pressure off entrenched power structures that would prefer to hoard local food supplies until rising prices can generate windfall profits. Free or cheap food must not become a prop for repressive governments who ignore the needs of their own people. The World Bank, the International Monetary Fund, and other lending institutions must also change their loan strategies and refuse to fund development projects that promote commercial, export-oriented agriculture at the expense of farmers who produce staple foods for local markets. Export-oriented economic growth has essentially failed in the Third World, and more aid and expertise must be focused on small-scale projects of direct benefit to rural communities. The purpose of development funds should not be to open up new markets for the transnational corporations, nor should they be given to undemocratic regimes to improve the lives of the urban elite or to forestall political change or land reform. Local farmers must be consulted about their needs, and they must participate in the decisions that affect them.

The Small Farmer

Some would object that all this emphasis on the small food producer is misplaced, that it is modern commercial farming and the agribusiness network that provide the vast quantities of food and the means of distributing them that keep a crowded world alive, and that to return to a simpler kind of farming will reduce agricultural output and destroy the chances of underdeveloped nations to industrialize. The small farm, they will say, is a relic of the past, and no matter how painful the process is, millions of people must be forced out of farming as part of the natural transition from an agrarian society to an industrialized one. It is true that, in the history of the developed nations, millions of people were driven off the land to provide the labor force for the factories. But it is important to remember, especially in the United States during the late nineteenth century, that those workers were fed, not by corporate agriculture, but by a large number of relatively small, independent, and highly innovative family farmers. What we

Small farms continue to contribute to food production, in spite of corporate agriculture.

call the agribusiness system did not fully evolve until after our industrial takeoff, until after there were surpluses of food, and it was the result of specific decisions made by corporate interests, not the inherent low productivity of small farms.

Industrialization

Furthermore, in Third World nations, the poverty of rural people is a tremendous drag on development. Poverty doesn't simply mean that people are poor and hungry; it means that they cannot constitute a market for locally made consumer goods, and they cannot make a contribution to the growth of the economy or pay taxes to governments desperate for funds for investment in infrastructure. Large-scale commercial agriculture has brought in its wake control of development by foreign business interests. Given their debt burdens, the low prices for their exports, the high price of imported technology, and the austerity policies demanded by their creditors, no matter how many people are driven from the land, for the Third World nations, the factories will not come.

There is a kind of industrialization going on in the Third World, but it is based on exploiting the extreme poverty there by transferring manufacturing jobs to low-wage countries. Trade agreements that eliminate restrictions on foreign investment or that override local environmental and worker safety laws promote these transfers, which threaten standards of living in the developed nations. American workers are now in competition with workers in the *maquiladoras* in northern Mexico. Textile and apparel workers lose their jobs to child laborers in Honduras. This is simply a way of exploiting the urban poor, just as agribusiness exploits the rural poor, and of reorienting an underdeveloped nation's primitive industry toward cheap exports rather than domestic production. Workers who earn no more than a dollar a day for their labor are unlikely to become a prosperous urban middle class supporting a strong local economy.

Cheap labor and export-oriented industry also fueled the economic growth of the newly industrializing countries (NICs), the "tigers" of Southeast Asia—Taiwan, Singapore, Korea, and Hong Kong—and these countries are often put forward as examples of what underdeveloped nations can accomplish if they stay the course and follow Western models of development. But these countries thrived under a very special set of historical circumstances. During the Cold War and the war in Vietnam, they received enormous amounts of American aid as front-line bulwarks against communism. They also received heavy investments and technology transfers from Japan, which was trying to escape its own rising labor costs. They did not practice free trade, but closed their markets as much as possible to foreign imports. And they had a ready market for their manufactures in the United States, which in the 1960s and 1970s was less concerned than it is today with East Asian imports. Authoritarian governments kept wages down, and cheap labor was sustained by controls on farm prices, which kept the cost of food low. Today, the rising cost of labor in these countries is forcing Taiwanese and Korean corporations to transfer their operations to even lower-wage countries like China, Malaysia, Thailand, and Indonesia, and the United States is engaged in a trade war to reduce imports from the NICs and to force them to open up their markets to Western goods. All the signs indicate that the rapid economic growth of the Southeast Asian tigers is slowing down, and in 1998 their economies collapsed. It is debatable whether these nations offer a useful model for other underdeveloped countries.

Free Trade and Free Markets

Free trade must become fair trade. Wherever there are great differences in the economic power of nations, unrestricted trade only permits the developed nations to flood the underdeveloped nations with manufactured goods, destroying local industries. During the colonial period, cheap imported English textiles put thousands of weavers and craftsmen out of work in India. Free trade and privatization schemes allow foreign investors to take over local economies and transform them for the production of goods that are of little benefit to the people. Foreign investors have the capital to do so; who among the poor can purchase a bank or a power company that a Third World government is forced to sell off? In negotiating free-trade agreements, it may be necessary to maintain protections for local industries producing for local markets, if modernization is ever to take place. Trade agreements must be based on the ability of all participating nations to market goods of equal value to each other. And there must be restrictions on the exploitation of cheap labor. All this, of course, goes against the theory of free markets.

Free markets are wonderful mechanisms for encouraging competition and innovation, forces that an industrialized nation is better prepared to cope with, but free markets also tend to marginalize the poor. The prices of commodities will always stabilize at some point above that which can be paid by millions of the lowest-income consumers. It is one thing for some consumers to accept the fact that they cannot afford the latest model television set, refrigerator, or luxury car. It is quite another thing for consumers to realize that they cannot afford enough food. The industrialized nations are rich enough to provide welfare programs and income supplements to marginalized consumers, and yet their development strategies for the poorer nations demand reductions in government subsidies and price controls. This practice must be stopped. Nations that refuse to follow the free-market model, especially on the issue of food self-sufficiency, must not be demonized and politically isolated.

If we keep the above general principles in mind when we evaluate the policies of governments, the changes in world trading patterns, the activities of agribusiness, and the strategies of development banks, we should have a fairly effective means of deciding whether or not real efforts are being made to deal with the problems of the poor and hungry. If we are to solve all the technical problems associated with global hunger and provide food for a growing world population, the urgent tasks are not technical. The food producers of the world need land reform, adequate employment and income, debt relief, greater control over the economic forces that affect their daily lives, greater access to resources, less dependence on decisions made by merchants and industrialists in distant places, and the one thing upon which all these other things depend—more democracy so that the voices of the food producers are heard.

Source Notes

Chapter 2
1. Betty Fussell. *The Story of Corn* (New York: Knopf, 1994).
2. Gwynne Dyer. *War* (New York: Crown, 1985), p. 4.

Chapter 3
1. John Ball, "The Sermon at Blackheath," 1381, cited in Susan George's *Ill Fares the Land* (London: Penguin, 1990).
2. Carson I. A. Ritchie. *Food in Civilization* (New York: Beaufort Books, 1981), p. 80.
3. Ibid., p. 138.

Chapter 4
1. Susan George. *How the Other Half Dies* (Totowa, NJ: Rowman & Allanheld, 1983).
2. Ibid.
3. Frances Moore Lappé. *Diet for a Small Planet*, revised edition (New York: Ballantine, 1991).
4. Susan George. *Ill Fares the Land* (London: Penguin, 1990).

Chapter 5
1. Francis Moore Lappé and Joseph Collins. *World Hunger: Twelve Myths* (New York: Grove Weidenfeld, 1986).
2. Tom Barry. *Roots of Rebellion* (Boston: South End Press, 1987).
3. Francis Moore Lappé and Joseph Collins with Cary Fowler. *Food First*, revised edition (New York: Ballantine, 1978).
4. Michael Maren, "The Food-Aid Racket," *Harper's* (August 1993).

Chapter 6
1. Cary Fowler and Pat Mooney. *Shattering: Food, Politics, and the Loss of Genetic Diversity* (Tucson: University of Arizona Press, 1990).

2. Walter H. Corson, editor. *The Global Ecology Handbook* (Boston: Beacon Press, 1990).
3. Ibid.
4. Francis Moore Lappé and Joseph Collins. *World Hunger: Twelve Myths* (New York: Grove Weidenfeld, 1986).
5. Muhammad Yunus, speech at the World Bank Conference on overcoming global hunger (Washington, D.C., November 1993).

For Further Information

Books

Barry, Tom. *Roots of Rebellion* (Boston: South End Press, 1987).
———. *Zapata's Revenge* (Boston: South End Press, 1995).
Bello, Walden. *Dark Victory: The United States, Structural Adjustment, and Global Poverty* (Oakland, CA: Institute for Food and Development Policy [Food First], 1994).
Bello, Walden, and Stephanie Rosenfeld. *Dragons in Distress: Asia's Miracle Economies in Crisis* (Oakland, CA: Institute for Food and Development Policy [Food First], 1992).
Branford, Sue, and Bernardo Kucinski. *The Debt Squads* (London: Zed Books, 1988).
Braudel, Fernand. *The Structures of Everyday Life. Volume I: Civilization and Capitalism, 15th–18th Century* (New York: Harper & Row, 1979).
Burbach, Roger, and Patricia Flynn. *Agribusiness in the Americas* (New York: Monthly Review Press, 1990).
Cherrington, Mark. *Degradation of the Land* (New York: Chelsea House, 1992).
Corson, Walter H., editor. *The Global Ecology Handbook* (Boston: Beacon Press, 1990).

Curwen, E. Cecil, and Gudmund Hatt. *Plough and Pasture* (New York: Henry Schuman, 1953).

Cushing, D. H. *The Provident Sea* (Cambridge: Cambridge University Press, 1988)

Dawson, Imogen. *Food and Feasts in the Middle Ages* (New York: New Discovery Books, 1994).

Doyle, Jack. *Altered Harvest* (New York: Viking Penguin, 1985).

Fox, Michael W. *Agricide* (New York: Schocken Books, 1986).

Fowler, Cary, and Pat Mooney. *Shattering: Food, Politics, and the Loss of Genetic Diversity* (Tucson: University of Arizona Press, 1990).

Fussell, Betty. *The Story of Corn* (New York: Knopf, 1994).

George, Susan. *The Debt Boomerang* (London: Pluto Press, 1992).

———. *A Fate Worse Than Debt* (London: Penguin, 1988).

———. *How the Other Half Dies* (Totowa, NJ: Rowman & Allanheld, 1983).

———. *Ill Fares the Land* (London: Penguin, 1990).

Hardeman, N. *Shucks, Shocks, and Hominy Blocks* (Baton Rouge: Louisiana State University Press, 1981).

Heiser, Charles B., Jr. *Seed to Civilization: The Story of Man's Food* (San Francisco: W. H. Freeman, 1973).

Howard, Robert West. *The Vanishing Land* (New York: Villard Books, 1985).

Johannessen, S., and C. A. Hastorf. *Corn and Culture in the Prehistoric New World* (Boulder, CO: Westview Press, 1994).

Lappé, Frances Moore. *Diet for a Small Planet*, revised edition (New York: Ballantine Books, 1991).

Lappé, Frances Moore, and Joseph Collins. *World Hunger: Twelve Myths* (New York: Grove Weidenfeld, 1986).

Lappé, Frances Moore, and Joseph Collins, with Cary Fowler. *Food First*, revised edition (New York: Ballantine Books, 1978).

Lappé, Frances Moore, Joseph Collins, and David Kinley. *Aid as Obstacle* (San Francisco: Institute for Food and Development Policy, 1981).

Loftas, Tony, editor. *Dimensions of Need* (Rome: United Nations Food and Agriculture Organization, 1995).

McClung, Kathleen. *Hungry for Justice* (Oakland, CA: Institute for Food and Development Policy [Food First], 1996).

Miller, G. Tyler, Jr. *Living in the Environment* (Belmont, CA: Wadsworth, 1990).
Morgan, Dan. *Merchants of Grain* (New York: Viking, 1979).
Paulsen, Gary. *Farm: A History and Celebration of the American Farmer* (Englewood Cliffs, NJ: Prentice-Hall, 1977).
Raskin, Edith. *World Food* (New York: McGraw Hill, 1971).
Ritchie, Carson I. A. *Food in Civilization* (New York: Beaufort, 1981).
Roddick, Jackie. *The Dance of the Millions* (London: Latin American Bureau, 1988).
Rodney, Walter. *How Europe Underdeveloped Africa* (London: Bogle-L'Ouverture, 1972).
Rothschild, Brian J. *Global Fisheries* (New York: Springer-Verlag, 1983).
Smith, Bruce D. *The Emergence of Agriculture.* Scientific American Library (New York: W. H. Freeman, 1995).
Wilson, C. Anne. *Food and Drink in Britain from the Stone Age to Recent Times* (London: Constable, 1973).

Internet Sites

Center for Integrated Agriculture Systems,
University of Wisconsin-Madison
http://www.wisc.edu./cias/

Website for this institute that studies farming practices, farm profitability, the environment, and rural vitality. Provides information on staff, research, publications, and links to related sites and discussion groups.

Center for Sustaining Agriculture and Natural Resources,
Washington State University
http://csnar.wsu.edu/

Webiste for this organization that addresses issues, practices, and technologies relating to agriculture and natural resource viability. Provides information about projects, programs, and related sites.

Food and Agriculture Organization (FAO) of the United Nations
http://www.fao.org

Contains much valuable information about United Nations efforts and programs to alleviate hunger worldwide.

Food First
http://www.foodfirst.org
Founded by Francis Moore Lappé, author of Diet for a Small Planet, *the Institute for Food and Development Policy, or Food First, is a leading food think tank and activist organization working to empower the hungry to bring about economic and political change.*

Hunger Web
http://www.brown.edu/Departments/World_Hunger_Program
Sponsored by the World Hunger Program of the Watson Institute of International Studies at Brown University.

National Food Safety Initiative
http://vm.cfsan.fda/gov/~dms/fs-toc.html
Sponsored by the Food and Drug Administration, U.S. Department of Agriculture, U.S. Environment Protection Agency, and the Centers for Disease Control and Prevention, this site offers information about produce safety, inspections, education, research, and other aspects of food safety.

Second Harvest
http://www.secondharvest.org/
Homepage for the largest domestic hunger relief organization in the United States. Discusses the problem of hunger, how Second Harvest works, and what volunteers can do to help.

The USDA National Hunger Clearinghouse
http://www.iglou.com/why/usda.htm
Managed by the U.S. Department of Agriculture, this site facilitates the sharing of information about world hunger with a database of more than 30,000 organizations.

Index

Numbers in *italics* refer to illustrations.

Adrian, Pope, 162
Agincourt, Battle of, 53
Agribusiness, 108, 135–139, 150–153
Agriculture, 19, 30–32, 33–40, 45–67, 71–77, 94–97
    commercial, 104–107
    early farming, 45–47
    fertilizers, 185–187
    harvest, 42, 44, 47, 66
    land use, 182–183
    in the New World, 61–64
    pesticides, 185–187
    productivity, 187–188
    small farmer, 193–195, *194*
    in the United States, 106
    water management, 183–185
Aid to foreign countries. *See* Food aid.
Alexander the Great, 67
Allen, Grant, 40
Allied Mills, 136
Altered Harvest, 182
American Empire, 92–93
Appert, Nicolas, 100
Apples, 73
Arbenz, Jacobo, 137
Archeology, 30–31
Archer, George, 135
Archer-Daniels-Midland (ADM), 136
Armour, Philip, 98

Bacteria, 28, 33, 176–178
Baker, Lorenzo Dow, 92, 137
Banquets, 69–70, 76
Ball, John, 72
Barry, Tom, 151
Bay of Pigs invasion, 137
Beauvilliers, Antoine, 101
Beer, 47, 54, 62, 73, 76
Bering Strait, 61
Black, Eli, 137
Black Death, 66, 74, 77
Bligh, Captain William, 90–91

Bonaparte, Napoleon, 91, 99–100
A Book for All Housekeepers, 100
Borden, Gail, 100, 117
Borlaug, Norman, 127
Boston Fruit Company, 137
Bounty (ship), 90–91
Bread, 14, 17, 54, 62, 70, 72, 73
Breast milk, 17
Breeding animals, 30, 48–50, 63
Breeding plants, 126–129
Brillat-Savarin, Anthelme, 101
Bureau of Commercial Fisheries, 180

Caesar, Julius, 69, 70
Cain, 50, *51*
Calcium, 16, 17, 109
Calgene, 128
Cambrian explosion, 23
Carbohydrates, 12, 17, 36
Cargill, 135–136, 160
Carver, George Washington, 123
Castro, Fidel, 137
Cattle, *15*, 16, 49, 55, 73, 81, *115*, 179–180. *See also* Meat.
    wild, 28, 56
Celanese, 181
Ceres, 36, *37*
Charles I, 82
Childe, V. Gordon, 30
China, 39, 56–61, 64, 67, 77, 82
    land ownership, 60–61
    natural disasters, 60
    starvation in, 66
Chin Shih Huang, 59
Chiquita Brands International, 93, 137–138
Chocolate, 87–89
Christianity, 71
Ciba-Geigy, 181
Cicero, 69
City-states, 64–67
Clay, Henry, 116
Climate, 40, 45
Clinton, Bill, 138
Coffee, 87–89

Coffeehouses, *88*, 89
Collins, Joseph, 142, 146, 167, 188
Columbus, Christopher, 81
Conasupo, 171
Conflict. *See* Warfare.
Confucianism, 60, 65
Connolly, James, 165
Continental Grain Company, 136
Cook, Captain James, 86
Cooking, 9, 28–29
Cornell University, 162
Cortés, Hernán, 87
Creation, 31
Crecy, Battle of, 53
Cretors, Charles, 126
Cromwell, Oliver, 164

Da Gama, Vasco, 82
Dairy, 17, 49
      production of, 114–121
Daniels, John, 136
Darwin, Charles, *34*, 35
Davis, John H., 108
Debt, 154–159, 190–193
Deere, John, 97, 190
De Gotari, Carlos Selina, 171
Delmonico, Lorenzo, 103
Diet for a Small Planet, 16, 121
Dickens, Charles, 146
Digestion, 17, 23, 29
Diu, Battle of, 82
Dole (company), 137
Dole, James, 92
Domestication, 39
Donkin, Bryan, 100
Doyle, Jack, 182
Drake, Francis, 84
Drought, 166–167, *166*
Dumont, René, 121
Dutch East India Company, 84–85

EEC. *See* European Economic Community.
Eland, 178–179, *179*
Emperors, 59–60
Erlich, Anne H., 145
Erosion, 35, 182–183
Escoffier, Georges-Auguste, 102
European Economic Community (EEC), 152
Evolution, 33
Experience of food, 7–10

Famine, 10, 60, 65–66, 162–168. *See also* Hunger.

Farming. *See* agriculture.
Feasting, 69–70, 76
Ferdinand, King of Spain, 81
Fertile Crescent, 45, *46*, 48, 49, 52, 53, 59, 67, 69
Fertilization, 63, 185–187
Feudalism, 60, 71–79
Fiber, 17, 176
Fire, 28, 43
First humans, 26–61
Fish, 16, 17, 24, 64, 82, 109–114
      in rice paddies, 58
Fishing, 28, 109–114
Fish protein concentrate, 180
Flavr Savr, 128
Food aid, 159–162
Food and Agriculture Organization of the United
      Nations, 124, 142, 182
Food and Drug Administration, 117, 128
Food pyramid, 17, *18*
Fox, Charles, 91
Frazer, Sir James George, 41–42
Fribourg, Simon, 136
Frito-Lay, 128
Fruits, 14, 17, 19, 26, 29, 35, 45, 59, 73, 99, 176
Fussell, Betty, 42

Garden of Eden, 31
GATT. *See* General Agreement on Tariffs and
      Trade.
General Agreement on Tariffs and Trade (GATT),
      134, 152
Genetics, 43–45
George, Susan, 120, 130
Global Tomorrow Coalition, 182, 187
Glucose, 12, 22
The Golden Bough, 41–42
Gonzales, Barrera Roberto, 172
Grains, 15, 16, 17, 29, 35, 36–47, 54–55, 56, 64,
      66, 69, 124–126, 176–178
      amaranth, 176
      barley, 14, 45, 47, 54, 69, 72
      cereal, 14, 17, 72
      corn, 14, 15, 16, 36, 45, 61–64, 66, 81, 82,
            125
      millet, 14, 56
      oats, 14, 72
      quinoa, *6*, *175*, 176
      rice, 14, 17, 36, 49, 57–58, 66, 124
      rye, 14, 72
      wheat, *13*, 14, 15, 36, 42, 45–47, 54, 66, 69,
            72, 124
Grameen (Village) Bank, 191–192

Grasses. *See* Grains.
Great Depression, 106
Green Revolution, The, 126–129
   in Mexico, 168–169
Grupo Industrial Maseca, 172

Harlan, Jack, R., 42
Hawkins, John, 84
Henry II, King of England, 162
Henry the Navigator, 82
History of food, 10–12, 20–32
Hood, Robin, 74
Hormones, bovine, 117
Horses, 59, 81, 101
   wild, 28
Howard, Robert West, 133
How the Other Half Dies, 120
Hunger, 8–9, 141–173. *See also* Famine.
Hunter-gatherers, 27, 28–29, 36, 38, 39–40, 45, 47, 61, 64

Ice age, 25–26
Ill Fares the Land, 130
Illinois, University of, 42
Illustrated London News, 165
IMF. *See* International Monetary Fund.
Industrialization, 195–196
Industrial Revolution, 94–98
Integrated Pest Management, 187
International Center for Improvement of Wheat and Maize (CIMMYT), 181
International Center for Living Aquatic Resources Management (ICLARM), 181
International Center of Tropical Agriculture (CIAT), 180
International Crops Research Institute for the Semi-Arid Tropics (ICRISAT), 180
International Food Policy Research Institute (IFPRI), 181
International Harvester, 190
International Institute of Tropical Agriculture (IITA), 181
International Livestock Research Institute (ILRI), 181
International Monetary Fund (IMF), 154, 156, 169, 193
International Plant Genetic Resources Institute (IPGRI), 181
International Potato Center (CIP), 181
International Rice Research Institute (IRRI), 127, 128, 180, 190

International Service for National Agriculture Research (ISNAR), 181
Irish potato famine, 162–165, *163*
IRRI. *See* International Rice Research Institute.
Irrigation, 54, 63, 64

Jefferson, Thomas, 95, *96*, 182
John Deere. *See* Deere, John.
Joseph (biblical), 66
Kublai Khan, 79

Land use, 182–183
Lappé, Francis Moore, 16, 121, 142, 146, 167, 188
Legumes, 14, 45, 61, 63, 121–123, 176–178
   beans, 15, 17, 54, 61, 63, 64, 81, 82
   nuts, 15, 16, 17, 26, 29, 35, 45, 61, 70, 81, 176
   soybeans, 15, 16, *122*
Light, 20, 22, 23
Lind, James, 85
Loans, 154–159
Louis XVI, 81
Louisiana State University, 128
Lovejoy, Thomas, 191
Lucullus, 69
Luther, Martin, 72

Magellan, Ferdinand, 82
Maize, 61–63. *See also* Grains/Corn.
Malthus, Thomas, 146
Maren, Michael, 162
Massey-Furguson, 190
Massilia, 67
McCormick, Cyrus, 97
Meat, 16, 17, 26, 49, 70, 73–74, 76, 82
   production of, 114–121
Mexico, 61–63, 168–173
Midland Linseed Products, 136
Monasteries (Christian), 74–76, *75*
Monsanto, 128, 181

NAFTA. *See* North America Free Trade Agreement.
Narcotics, 93–94
National Geographic, 167
Natural selection, 24, 43
Newly industrializing countries (NICs), 196
New York Times, The, 181
Non-government organizations (NGOs), 162
North America Free Trade Agreement (NAFTA), 134, 152, 171, 172

Nutrition, 8–9, 12–19
    at sea, 85–86

Occidental Petroleum, 181
Olin, 181
Opium, 93–94
Organization of Petroleum Exporting Companies (OPEC), 129
Overseas Shipping Group, 136

Palmerson, Lord, 165
Pesticides, 185–187
Pigs, 45, 52, 58, 61, 81, 119. *See also* Meat.
    wild, 28, 48
Pioneer Hi-Bred Corn Company, 127, 181
Pirie, N. W., 177
Plant Variety Protection Act, 181
Polo, Marco, 79, 81
Pompey, 69
Population, 141–146
Potatoes, 14, 61, 63, 81–82
Poultry, 16, 17, 64
    chickens, 16, 58, 61, 119
    ducks, 55, 70
    turkey, 42, 45, 64
Poverty, 146–149
Preservatives, 130–135
Preserving food, 99–100
Preston, Andrew, 137
Price of food, 1139–140
Private voluntary organizations (PVOs), 162
Production of food, 19, 108–109, 130–139

Quaker Oats, 136

Raleigh, Sir Walter, 82, *83*
Ralston Purina Company, 138, 160
Records, written, 32
Redenbacher, Orville, 126
Reform, 188–190
Religion, 40–42, 65, 116
Restaurants, 101
Rituals, 40–42, 65
Roman Catholics, 72
Roman Empire, 67–70, 74
    feasts, *68*, 69–70
Rome, 71–72
    starvation in, 66
Roots of Rebellion, 151
Royal Dutch Shell, 181
Ruckheim, Frederick William and Louis, 126

Sacrificial animals, 40–42, *41*
Salinas family, 172
Sara Lee Corporation, 138
Scott, Captain Robert Falcon, 86
Scurvy, 17, 86
Seeds, 26, 29, 35, 36–38, 39, 40, 42–43, 45, 47, 176–178
Settlements, 42–43
Sheep, 16, 45, 55. *See also* Meat.
    wild, 28, 48
Shen Nung, 87
Single-celled organisms, 22–23
Skinner, Curtis, 142
Slavery, 91
Social Policy, 142
Social status, 10–12
Spice Islands, 82
Spices, 59, 70, 77, 79, 81–85, 86
Stanford University, 145
Staples, 14
Starches, 12, 36, 123–124
Starvation, 8–9, 14, 65–66
    at sea, 85
Storage of food, 42–43
The Story of Corn, 42
Sugar, 12, 22, 76, 87, 89–92
Sugar cane, 59, 81, 89, 92
Sumptuary laws, 73–74
Sunlight. *See* light.
Swift, Gustavus, 98

Tea, 87–89
Technology, 101–104
Tilling. *See* Agriculture.
Tipperary Vindicator, 165
Townsend, Viscount, 95
Trade, 77–91, 134–139, 153–154, 196–198
Transnational companies, 135–139
Transporting food, 98–99
A Treatise on Scurvy, 85
Trollope, Anthony, 97
Tull, Jethro, 95
Tyson, Don, 138
Tyson Foods, 138

United Fruit Company, 93, 137
United Nations Convention on the Law of the Sea, 112
United States, 64, 92–93
Unites States Centers for Disease Control, 118
Urban, Thomas, 181

Urbanization, 101–104
Upjohn Company, 128, 181

Vanishing Land, The, 133
Vegetables, 14, 16, 17, 19, 54
Vitamins, 16–17, 36, 47, 64, 84–85, 109

Wallace, Henry A., 127
Walpole, Robert, 95
Warfare, 50–56, 64–66
Washington, George, 91
Water, 17, 39, 56, 63, 79
Water management, 183–185
Wealth, 43, 49, 67–70, 73, 74, 146–149
Weapons, 28–29
Wellesley, Sir Arthur, 100

Wellington, Duke of, 100
West African Rice Development Association in Bouaké (WARDA), 181
Whitney, Eli, 97
William III, King of England, 164
Wine, 70, 76
Winemaking, 67
  in monasteries, 74–76
Wood, Charles, 164
World Bank, 154, 156, 193
World Hunger, 142, 188
World Wildlife Fund, 191

Yunas, Muhammad, 191–192

Zemurray, Samuel, 137

About the Author

Jake Goldberg, who lives in New York City, is a writer and editor of young adult books. He has written two previous books for Franklin Watts, *Albert Einstein: The Rebel Behind Relativity* and *The Disappearing American Farm*.